Is God DONE *with* America?

RABBI ERIC CARLSON

NEW YORK

Is God DONE *with* America?

by RABBI ERIC CARLSON
© 2011 Rabbi Eric Carlson. All rights reserved.

ISBN 978-1-60037-876-8 Paperback
ISBN 978-1-60037-877-5 EPub Version
Library of Congress Control Number: 2010938743

Published by:

MORGAN JAMES PUBLISHING
The Entrepreneurial Publisher
5 Penn Plaza, 23rd Floor
New York City, New York 10001
(212) 655-5470 Office
(516) 908-4496 Fax
www.MorganJamesPublishing.com

Cover Design by:
Rachel Lopez
rachel@r2cdesign.com

Interior Design by:
Bonnie Bushman
bbushman@bresnan.net

In an effort to support local communities, raise awareness and funds, Morgan James Publishing donates one percent of all book sales for the life of each book to Habitat for Humanity.
Get involved today, visit
www.HelpHabitatForHumanity.org.

Dedication

I wish to dedicate this Heavenly Tome to my Jewish Messiah, Yeshua, and my beautiful wife Barbara. The two most important people in my life. Yeshua, ever faithful and patient, stayed with me and never gave up on me when I spent numerous years in the wilderness, running from my heavenly calling and destiny.

My wife Barbara was the source and inspiration for my return to Service of the King almost 20 years ago. My life has made many transformations in these last 16 years. With great love, understanding, affection, and discernment my best friend, my soul mate, my wife has been a continuous source of support, strength, and inspiration to me. This work would not have been possible without her. Thank you Yeshua, thank you Barb!

Acknowledgments

I wish to give special acknowledgment to Senior Pastor Bob Collins of the World Outreach Worship Center in Newport News, VA. Who has been a patient teacher, mentor, and a "Roman Centurion" who so loves the Jewish people that he has allowed our congregation to meet in his churches facilities for over 10 years.

I wish to acknowledge Sid Roth of Messianic Vision who is a spiritual Father and mentor to me. He discerned my calling before I knew I had one!

I give special thanks to Anthony S. Mulford, Esq. and Peter A Shaddock II Esq. who gave me sound, biblical based legal counsel that guided me through the complicated publishing process.

"Where there is no counsel, plans fail; But in a multitude of counselors they are established." Proverbs 15:22

I wish to thank Coach Bill McCartney and Dr. Raleigh Washington of Promise Keepers, benefactors of the Messianic Movement and champions of truth. May the Lord God of Israel bless you and keep you!

To the "Wolf Pack", Chief Anne and Pastor Wade, I am blessed to be in covenant with you. We have enjoyed many good hunts together with many more yet to come!

I also with to thank Garnette Doggett who sacrificed her time and talent to edit this manuscript and find the multitude of errors I had made. You are a blessing! Thank you!

Eric S Carlson, Rabbi

Table of Contents

iii   Dedication

v   Acknowledgments

ix   Preface

xi   Foreword by Sid Roth

1   Chapter 1: America, the Land of the Free!

11   Chapter 2: Silence is a Sin

25   Chapter 3: Messianic Israel

51   Chapter 4: The First Body

69   Chapter 5: America's Prophetic Destiny as a Nation

81   Chapter 6: The Olive Tree

91   Chapter 7: The Restoration of All Things!

91   Chapter 8: What Does God Want Me to Do?

133   Rabbi Eric & Barb Carlson

135   APPENDIX A

Preface

Josh McDowell, Barna's Christian Statistics and many other resources have painted a very dower and bleak statistical portrait of a dead and dying church in America today. Powerless and ineffective at influencing greater society, the body of Messiah in America is in retreat and losing ground daily on all fronts. The number one growing religion in America today is Islam! America is in a crisis!

A faithful remnant of Jewish and Gentile believers are obediently seeking the face of God. They are inquiring of the Ruach HaKodesh (Holy Spirit) and desperately seeking God in this hour. This intercession has revealed a great urgency, a cry out to God for His intervention into a morally corrupt and bankrupt America.

Dr. Michael Brown's book "Revolution" and James Rutz's book "Mega Shift" accurately record this urgency and reveal that a major paradigm shift is currently occurring within the body of Messiah. This paradigm shift is a restoration and return to biblical truth in preparation for the return of the Jewish Groom, Yeshua.

Scripture records God's strategy to infuse life back into the dead church or "Life from the Dead". As you read on and learn this strategy remember that God holds you accountable to what you know.

> *"Now the servant who knew what his master wanted but didn't prepare or act according to his will, will be whipped with many lashes;* [48]*however, the one who did what deserves a beating, but didn't know, will receive few lashes. From him who has been given much, much will be demanded—from someone to whom people entrust much, they ask still more".*
> **Luke 12:47-48**

To know God's word, commands, and desires and remain disobedience is rebellion, the sin of witchcraft. What does God want in this hour? Its recorded in His written word, the Bible! Will you be obedient to God's word and will?

Foreword
by Sid Roth

The future of worldwide revival is tied to Israel. And the future of America is tied to Israel. It is no accident that "USA" is found in the center of Jer-USA-lem.

The pivotal Scripture for America's survival (or for the survival of any nation) is Obadiah 1:15:

"For the day of the LORD upon all nations is near; as you have done [to Israel], it shall be done to you."

The law of evangelism has always been to evangelize the Jew first. When God wanted to reach the world, He went to the Jew first, Abraham. When Jesus wanted to evangelize the world, He went to the Jew first (Matt. 15:24). And when Paul, the apostle to the Gentiles, wanted to evangelize the world, he too went to the Jew first (Rom. 1:16). I have found as I have practiced the law of evangelism throughout the world that I have reached more Gentiles than if I had gone to the Gentile first.

The way to reach the Jew is through signs and wonders (1 Cor. 1:22). The people whom God has chosen

to evangelize the Jew are the Gentiles (Rom. 11:11b).
This is why God is now equipping Gentiles to move in
extraordinary signs and wonders.

As the Jewish people join believing Gentiles as part of the
body of Messiah, it will form the "One New Man" described
by Paul in Ephesians 2:14-16. This in turn will lead to a great
worldwide revival. Amos 9 says there will be a great harvest
when the tabernacle of David is restored. The word "tabernacle"
in Hebrew means "house" or "family." In other words, when the
family of David (the Jewish people) is restored to God, it will usher
in the greatest Gentile revival in history.

This is the set time to favor Zion (Israel). Jewish people are
more open to the gospel now than at any time I have seen in over
30 years of Jewish ministry. It is God's time to evangelize the Jew.

"He who gathers in summer is a wise son; he who sleeps
in harvest is a son who causes shame" (**Prov. 10:5**).

I have known Rabbi Eric Carlson for 11 years. He has taken
my concepts on the One New Man and pioneered one of the best
One New Man congregations in the country. I expect him to go
even further than I have with the end-time One New Man move
of God.

Is God Done with America? will give you the Kingdom reason
God has called America into existence and blessed it more than
any nation in history. As you read and understand the book, God
will use you to usher in America's greatest days in history.

Unless otherwise noted all scripture quoted from the "Complete Jewish Bible" Translated by Dr. David Stern.

Complete Jewish Bible

Jewish New Testament Publications, Inc.
P.O. Box 615, Clarksville, Maryland 21209. USA
Copyright 1998

Chapter 1

America, the
Land of the Free!

I. Crossroads.

The Republic of America is currently at a spiritual and physical crossroads. Most of America's citizens are unaware of this crossroads and the urgency of the hour and the path to take. America was founded over 400 years ago by men and women who loved and followed the living God of Israel, the God of Abraham, Isaac, and Jacob! God was the center and focus of their writings, their work, and the government they founded. God's word is the source foundation from which the United States Constitution was written[1]. America was and remains a place where various cultures and ideas from around the world mix freely and live together under one nation, under one God, indivisible, with liberty and justice for all! There is literally no other nation on the earth like the United States of America.

Americas Godly foundations and principles were seeded by Great Britain, America's mother country. English principles of law such as the revolutionary "Magna Carta" written in the 13th century were an antecedent to the Unites States Consitution[2]. The radical writings of John Locke, an 18th century Scottish physician and political philosopher also greatly influenced the writers of the U.S. Constitution. Locke's radical thoughts about individual's freedom to worship God and forms of self-government of the people and by the people are a significant source of America's concept of bible based freedom, liberty, and God given inalienable rights for every person[3].

Here's the point I wish to make with this short digression into American History. The Republic of America was formed upon a relationship with the God of Israel[1] which explains why America is a Republic vice a Democracy. Our Founding Fathers were solid, bible based believers in Yeshua, the actual Hebrew name of Jesus which is the term America's founders used 400 years ago. This is why the U.S. Constitution never once mentions the term "democracy"[4]. A republic is based upon the biblical principle that humanity has been granted certain inalienable rights by God such as life, liberty, and the pursuit of happiness. Life is a gift from God alone. A republic is a national government established to protect those God given, inalienable rights of its citizen. The republic doesn't establish rights; the rights are given to us by God. The republic only protects those rights.

A democracy, which is how America is referred to today, is a form of government in which the government or state determines individual rights, not God. Ancient Greece and Rome were democracies[5]. This is a subtle yet dramatic and drastic difference. America has strayed from its roots as a Judeo/Christian republic by following the destructive paths of the Ancient Greek and Roman democratic empires. America is turning away from its covenant with the God of Abraham, Isaac, and Jacob established at its birth.

This is the same God who established America and gave us our inalienable rights.

Despite Americas mistakes and shortcomings in its beginning (genocide of the First Nations inhabitants for their land and natural resources and Slavery to name a few) God blessed America because it sought after and feared God. America was a nation filled with God fearing people who maintained their covenant relationship with Him. America gave these same rights to its Jewish citizens which blessed America in accordance with God's promise through Abraham.

> *"I will bless those who bless you, but I will curse anyone who curses you; and by you all the families of the earth will be blessed."* **Genesis 12:3**

America established and maintained a biblical, marriage type covenant relationship with God and now in modern times with the Nation of Israel because America was founded and governed by biblical principle. A United States Supreme Court ruling " THE UNITED STATES SUPREME COURT HOLY TRINITY CHURCH v. U.S. 143 U.S. 457, 12 S.Ct. 511, 36 L.Ed. 226 Feb. 29, 1892 stated that America was a Christian Nation based upon the bible which influenced our founding fathers and their Colonial charters, the Mayflower pack, the Declaration of Independence, and the Federal and Individual States Constitutions.

II. Adultery

Over the course of the last five decades America's financial foundation departed from the gold standard which was replaced with black gold, the oil standard in 1971[6]. This financial, economic, and political shift caused a moral and ethical dilemma for the nation. America's established covenant relationship with God was being challenged. The greed for more profits caused America to commit adultery with the God of Israel by coming into a covenant relationship with Islam and Allah, the god of Ishmael who had control of the crude oil that America desired. America strayed from its Judeo/Christian covenant, tempted by the secular and strategic need for crude oil. There are always consequences for actions taken. It's interesting to note that when America forced Israel to vacate the Gaza strip and turn control over to the Palestinians, God struck the heart of America's oil empire, the Louisiana Gulf coast with Hurricane Katrina followed by hurricane Rita, both in 2005. These hurricanes shut down oil production for weeks which caused retail gas prices in America to quadruple! God revealed himself to America by coming against their god just as he did in Egypt over 3,700 years ago by coming against their gods with the ten plagues!

A nation cannot be in covenant with the God of Israel and the god of Ishmael, Allah. America is no exception to this rule. God calls this type of relationship adultery and idolatry. God has clearly established and defined America as a Godly nation, not a Muslim nation. America was founded in covenant with the God of Israel. This book is a clarion call to the greater body of Messiah in America to hear the Watchman's Shofar and awaken from its slumber. America must understand its biblical roots and turn back to God before judgment falls. America has not yet fulfilled its Godly, prophetic destiny as a nation, the reason God raised up America!

III. The Balfour Declaration.

America is not the first nation and superpower to face this type of geopolitical and spiritual crossroad regarding Israel. Before America, the world's Super Power was Great Britain who held the position until the end of World War II. For the previous 100 years the sun never set on the British Empire. Great Britain was the world's largest empire ever recorded to date. For most of the 19th century and almost half of the 20th century Great Britain governed one third of the world's population (about 458 million people)[7]. England ruled the seven seas with its great fleet of warships and held sovereign control over lands in every continent, 13,000,000 square miles, approximately twenty five percent of the earth's land mass[7]. Most of Great Britain's citizens and leaders during this period of history were devout, God fearing Christians. Great Britain had experienced wave upon wave of revival! God poured out His spirit upon them and their nation. These revivals began with the great Methodist movement through John Wesley and culminated in the great Welsh Revival led by Evans Roberts in 1905 which brought well over 150,000 people to faith. This great revival spread throughout Europe, Africa, India, Australia, China, Canada, Russia, and was the seed of America's Azusa Street outpouring in 1906[8].

This great outpouring of God's Spirit transformed the people and leaders of Great Britain to understand God's heart; a strong and zealous love for Israel and the Jewish people. This revelation swept through the British Empire, spawned from this great revival at the beginning of the 20th century. Theodore Herzl, the world's first Zionist and champion for the restoration of Israel as a nation found great favor in the British Parliament during this time of revival. Prior to World War I Israel was under geo-political control of the Muslim based "Ottoman Turkish Empire".

In 1914 World War I began with the assassination of Archduke Franz Ferdinand of Austria[9]. As the war spread across Europe, the population witnessed the most horrendous wholesale slaughter of men the European Continent had ever experienced to date. Engaged in trench warfare, Great Britain and its ally France were in a stalemate against the Austrian/Hungarian/Ottoman Empire. For years both sides made advances measured in mere inches while they killed each other en masse with modern, powerful artillery and the newly invented machine gun. In April of 1917 America entered into the war, siding with Great Britain and France. Millions of soldiers and civilians died as Europe experienced the violent effects of this seemingly never ending war. Neither side could overcome the other's trenches.

Great Britain changed the tide of World War One with one invention, the Mechanized Tank[10]. These Tanks were heavily armored and armed vehicles on tracks. They were nicknamed land battleships. These tanks changed the tide and face of war forever. These tanks, powered by the recently invented diesel engine, had long, broad mechanical tracks that allowed the tank to easily drive over the tops of German trenches. The tank brought a relatively quick end to the war. Great Britain's victory meant the defeat and partition of the Ottoman Turkish Empire. The spoils of victory meant that Great Britain now assumed geo-political control and sovereignty over the entire Middle East region including the biblical land of Israel[11]. Their sovereignty over this region coupled with their God inspired love for Israel and their desire to reestablish Israel as a nation led to the Balfour Declaration of 1917, written the same year that World War I ended.

The Balfour Declaration, written by Great Britain's Foreign Secretary Arthur James Balfour, was a formal statement of policy by the British government which said:

> *"His Majesty's government view with favour the establishment in Palestine of a national home for the Jewish people, and will use their best endeavors to facilitate the achievement of this object, it being clearly understood that nothing shall be done which may prejudice the civil*

and religious rights of existing non-Jewish communities in Palestine, or the rights and political status enjoyed by Jews in any other country."

God poured out His Spirit upon Great Britain. He elevated them to the world's largest Empire ever recorded and blessed them with a resounding victory in World War I for His holy purpose and will; To restore the Nation of Israel according to His prophetic written word. God's purpose for Great Britain, their prophetic destiny and calling was to restore Israel as a Nation! But Great Britain fell short of God's will. Great Britain was tempted or seduced to pursue another path.

The seemingly minor historical event of the invention of the tank would change the known world forever. This new invention, the tank, was powered by another new invention, the diesel engine. Diesel engines run on diesel fuel. Great Britain has no natural oil resources. Their Godly destiny as a nation, as manifested through the Balfour Declaration was about to collide with their new found strategic need for oil resources. Great Britain was now sovereign over most of the Middle East territory that contained immense oil reserves. They flooded this area with their best geologists and major oil companies who began drilling and pumping the oil out of Iraq and Iran and into Great Britain[12]. A significant portion of the Middle East region, the area controlled by the descendants of Ishmael sat on top of the world's largest crude oil deposit ever discovered. Great Britain, who invented the tank and modern mechanized warfare strategically needed this oil for her new mechanized war machine. Great Britain began courting the descendents of Ishmael, the Arab people for their oil reserves.

Great Britain broke their promise contained in the Balfour Declaration in order to appease the Arab's for the crude oil they so desperately needed. Great Britain spiritually divorced themselves from Isaac and married Ishmael for oil. This change of heart and focus caused Great Britain to start a gradual downfall and decline as the world's largest Empire because they disobeyed God. The end of World War II in May of 1945 witnessed the sun setting on the British Empire. Great Britain ceased to be the world's largest Empire only Superpower. They lost sovereignty over most of their empire around the world and saw great economic decline as they struggled to repay the massive World War II debt they had accrued, all because they chose oil over God.

At the end of World War II God raised up another Superpower, the United States of America to stand with the Jewish People. Within eleven minutes of Israel declaring its independence on May 14th, 1948 then United States President Harry Truman, the leader of the world's most powerful nation, declared America's acknowledgment and support of the fledgling State of Israel[13]. At the same time great revival and an outpouring of God's Spirit unfolded in America. The revival and healing ministries of Jack Kemp Cole, Kathryn Kuhlman, and Billy Graham to name a few swept across American. Do you see the associative pattern here? America wasn't God's first choice to fulfill His word regarding Israel, Great Britain was! Great Britain failed to recognize their God ordained spiritual opportunity of a lifetime. When God's first choice wouldn't obey His will, God moved on to His second choice which was and currently is the United States of America. What a powerful lesson regarding God's grace and sovereignty!

Today, right now America is at the same exact crossroads Great Britain experienced at the end of World War I! America views the Middle East with great strategic interest for the same reason Great Britain did, oil. Maintaining a constant oil supply requires placating and appeasing the Muslim Nations who own the oil while seeking Israel's destruction. America is relying on worldly, secular agendas vice God's! Who will America choose to serve and please? The God of Abraham, Isaac, Jacob and the Jewish people or the god of Ishmael, Allah and the Muslim people. History will soon record the answer!

Chapter One Notes

1. "*What if Jesus Had Never Been Born*" by Dr. D. James Kennedy and Jerry Newcombe:

2. Charles Lund Black, "*A New Birth of Freedom*", 1999, p. 10, Yale University Press, ISBN 0-300-07734-3

3. Bailyn, Bernard, 1992 (1967). "*The Ideological Origins of the American Revolution*". Harvard Uni. Press

4. Review and actual copy of the Unites States Constitution at the U.S. Government sponsored WEB site: http://www.archives.gov/exhibits/charters/constitution.html

5. Grinin L. E. "Democracy and Early State. Social Evolution & History 3(2)", September 2004 (pp. 93-149

6. McNally, David. 2009. "*From financial crisis to world-slump: accumulation, financialisation, and the global slowdown.*" Historical Materialism.

7. Ferguson, Niall (2004). "*Empire.*" Basic Books. ISBN 0465023290.

8. J. Gwynfor Jones, "*Reflections on the Religious Revival in Wales 1904-05,*" "*Journal of the United Reformed Church History Society*", Oct 2005, Vol. 7 Issue 7, pp 427-445

9. Dejan Djokić. 'Yugoslavism: histories of a failed idea, 1918-1992". London, England, UK: C. Hurst & Co. Ltd, 2003.

10. Willmott, H.P. (2003), "*First World War*", Dorling Kindersley

11. Paul C. Helmreich, From Paris to Sèvres: "*The Partition of the Ottoman Empire at the Peace Conference of 1919-1920*" Publisher: Ohio Univ Pr

12. Daniel Yergin, The Prize: "*The Epic Quest for Oil, Money, and Power*", Simon and Schuster, 1991

13. President Truman's notes record he sign an acknowledgement of Israel as a state 11 minutes after Israel's declaration of Independence

   http://www.trumanlibrary.org/israel/palestin.htm

— Chapter 2 —

Silence is a Sin

I. Israel's Culture Influences America's Birth.

Israel is the only Nation on the earth whose culture, identity, and government is established and defined through a relationship with God. Israel's identity and culture centers on God and His word. "Torah" is a Hebrew word that means God's teachings that hit the mark. Torah is the first five books of the bible, Genesis, Exodus, Leviticus, Numbers, and Deuteronomy. Torah is God's heavenly constitution that establishes and outlines His Theocratic government, His Theocracy established here on earth for His people and those who choose to follow Him. This document, the Torah would not only change Israel, transforming a fragmented, loose knit tribal community into a nation worthy of His name. The Torah would forever change the course of human history, providing the foundational culture and government into which God's Son, Yeshua (Jesus) would be born. The Torah is the heavenly document by which God will judge the earth! Torah is heaven revealed to Man Kind. It is the foundation that establishes unity and peace among people and obedience to God, our King!

Numerous moral principles are taken directly from the Word of God and incorporated into the United States Constitution[1]. The founding fathers used the bible as their guide in all that they did. Each of the 13 original colonies experienced a loyalty of the people to that specific colony in which they lived. If you resided in Virginia in 1760 you were introduced as a Virginian. If you resided in Pennsylvania you were referred to as a Pennsylvanian and so on. When the taxes, tyranny, and oppression of Great Britain became overbearing the 13 colonies sent representatives to Philadelphia who founded the First Continental Congress in 1774. This body of delegates from every colony witnessed the transition of the 13 loose knit colonies into one cohesive nation. One of the most notable changes that occurred as a result of the Continental Congress was the term "American" replacing the previously used colonial reference[2]. As unity fostered among them, the colonists were no longer Virginian's or Pennsylvanian's, they referred to themselves simply as Americans! One of the most influential members of the Continental Congress and the one history records as responsible for their unity was Samuel Adams. The delegates from those 13 colonies were from varying Christian denominations. Let me add here that there were no Muslims in this country then. It was Christian with a relatively small contingent of Jewish people in America then. These various denominational backgrounds were unified through a common belief in the word of God. Sam Adams wrote the following statement about the convening of the Congress:

> *"Christian men, who had come together for solemn deliberation in the hour of their extremity, to say there was so wide a difference in their religious belief that they could not, as one man, bow a knee in prayer to the Almighty, whose advice and assistance they hoped to obtain.[3]"*

James Madison, the Chief architect of the U.S. Constitution, 4th President of the United States, and also a key member of that same Continental Congress stated in 1778:

"We have staked the whole future of American civilization, not upon the power of government, far from it. We have staked the future of all of our political institutions upon the capacity of mankind for self-government; upon the capacity of each and all of us to govern ourselves, to control ourselves, to sustain ourselves according to the Ten Commandments[3]*"*

George Washington (who should need no introduction here) wrote to his troops the following on July 9th, 1776:

"The General hopes and trusts that every officer and man, will endeavor so to live, and act, as becomes Christian soldiers defending the dearest Rights and Liberties of his country[3]*"*

Even Abraham Lincoln, the great emancipator who worked diligently to end the blight of slavery and guided the nation through its only civil war (which was fought over slavery) wrote this following thought to New Jersey State Senator James Scovel:

"Young Man, if God gives me four more years to rule this country, I believe it will become what it ought to be-what its Divine Author intended it to be-no longer one vast plantation for breeding human beings for the purpose of lust and bondage. But it will become a new valley of Jehoshaphat (Jezreel in Hebrew God Sows), where all nations of the earth will assemble together under one flag, worshipping a common God, and they will celebrate the resurrection of human freedom![3]*"*

America's birth is somewhat similar to Israel's birth. God spoke from Mt. Sinai to Moses and all Israel to reveal His absolute truth to them and command their obedience to it.

"You have seen what I did to the Egyptians, and how I carried you on eagles' wings and brought you to myself. [5]Now if you will pay careful attention to what I say and keep my covenant, then you will be my own treasure from among all the peoples, for all the earth is mine; [6]and you will be a kingdom of cohanim for me, a nation set apart. 'These are the words you are to speak to the people of Isra'el." [7]Moshe came, summoned the leaders of the people and presented them with all these words which ADONAI (Lord) had ordered him to say. [8]All the people answered as one, "Everything ADONAI has said, we will do." Moshe reported the words of the people to ADONAI." **Exodus 19:4-8**

This is the true model of covenant relationship God desires, those who are of one mind, in unity, to worship Him in Spirit and in Truth!

II. The Prophets.

God also raised up Prophets, Navi in Hebrew, to ensure strict compliance and obedience to His commands and written word. God employed these Navi primarily during periods in which Israel had strayed from God's word. Navi is a person designated by God as one who speaks forth for God.

Prophets is a Greek term for Navi. In the Greek a Prophet is a fortuneteller who spoke for god and interpreted god's word. The prophet would interpret the message of the Greek Delphi. In Greek mythology, Delphi was home of the Delphic oracle and the place of Apollo worship.

You may be wondering where I am going with this. What instigated Israel's Exodus from Egypt and their arrival at Mt Sinai 50 days later?

"Sometime during those many years the king of Egypt died, but the people of Isra'el still groaned under the yoke of slavery, and they cried out, and their cry for rescue from slavery came up to God. ²⁴God heard their groaning, and God remembered his covenant with Avraham, Yitz'chak and Ya'akov." **Exodus 2:22-24**

God heard Israel's cry and groaning and responds to their injustice. In Torah, God orders Israel DO NOT REMAIN SILENT in the FACE OF INJUSTICE! The prophets are sent by God to be His voice when He witnesses injustice. That's why God sent Moses, a Prophet! He heard Israel's cry!

"Do not go around spreading slander among your people, but also don't stand idly by when your neighbor's life is at stake; I am ADONAI." **Leviticus 19:16**

Remember God's words in Deuteronomy as well.

"Justice, only justice, you must pursue; so that you will live and inherit the land ADONAI your God is giving you." **Deuteronomy 16:20**

Israel had the liberty to accept or turn down God's offer of a covenant relationship which results in their freedom and liberty. The foundation of God's written word given to Israel at Mt Sinai are also the founding principles of the American Republic; Freedom, Liberty, and Justice! Liberty is a term that is often used in an offhand manner with few understanding its actual meaning. Liberty is freedom from physical restraint, freedom from arbitrary or despotic control. Liberty is the power of choice!

Liberty in America is endangered as the nation faces this crossroads of choice between the God of Israel or Islam. The silent majority need to become vocal and no longer remain silent. Iran, who most likely as I write this has a nuclear bomb and has openly voiced their desire to annihilate Israel yet the world, remains silent. The black tide of Islam and Shirah law is rising up all over the world and the world's free people remains silent, cowering in fear of upsetting Muslims while they torture and abuse women, forbid freedom of speech, behead Jews and Christians, and murder innocent people in the name of Islam. They perform Jihad through suicide bombings and the world remains silent. The black tide of Islam is taking over our cities, our schools and threatens the very document that provides our freedom and liberty as a nation; the Constitution of the United States of America. The majority of American News and Press agencies refuse to report the danger and truth of Radical Islam!

The sin of silence is a plaque that has infected America numerous times over the course of our history! Ask the victims of the "Peculiar Institution" (slavery) about freedom. Apathy and disregard did not free them; the sin of silence kept slavery alive in America long after it had been abolished in Great Britain and around the world. Finally, in the 1840's a strong abolitionist fever struck a few courageous people in the North and a strong moral resolve and conviction of a free people that all people, regardless of their skin color or race should be allowed to live in freedom led to our Civil War to remove the unsightly blight of slavery. It resulted in millions of oppressed African Americans being freed from the yoke of slavery. As Jews, we are empathetic and can relate to these former slaves regarding the oppression and hate they have suffered because we too were once slaves and oppressed by Egypt.

Adolph Hitler started the "Thousand Year Reich" in a very small and inconsequential manner. On 16 September 1919 he joined the German Workers' Party which had approximately forty members[3]. Shortly thereafter their name was changed to the

National Socialist German Workers' Party and by July 1921 Hitler was its chairman. How, you may ask did this heinous murderer of humanity who authored the death of over six million Jews and millions more Europeans become the supreme Chancellor of Germany twelve short years later? The same Germany that before Hitler was Europe's greatest democracy, with the world's greatest universities that produced the likes of Albert Einstein who discovered the "Theory of Relativity", Wernher von Braun the rocket scientist who NASA and America's space program was built around, Leo Szilard the driving force behind the development of America's Atomic Bomb to name just a few. Hitler came to this position of power because an apathetic society chose not to challenge him, they remained silent! Think how easy it would have been to stop Hitler and the Nazi's when they were less than 50 in numbers and meeting in a beer hall. Think how many millions of lives, Americans, European, and Jews would have been saved if Hitler had not been ignored and confronted instead of the world remaining silent! The Church, afraid to upset the apple cart remained silent throughout Europe and even in America during the Holocaust. Separation of Church and state philosophy cost some 60 million lives in WW II. Granted, there were a few German Pastors who spoke out such as Dietrich Bonhoeffer and Martin Niemoller but they were few in numbers and easily found, arrested, and sent to the death camps. What if every European Pastor had taken a stand and spoken out against the Nazi's? What if every European Christian had said "No, you're not taking our Jewish brothers and sisters" to Nazi's? What if every Rabbi had resisted, what if the Church had resisted the Nazi's? What if the German people themselves had not remained silent and resisted Hitler? History could have recorded a vastly different story and literally millions of lives could have been spared!

III. Why is the body of Messiah silent?

"All that is necessary for evil to triumph is for good
men to do nothing!" — *Edmund Burke*

How does Anti-Semitism happen in our world today when
we have a complete and comprehensive History to teach us? How
is it that we are fighting a religious war with Islam and the world
is sympathetic with Islam (whose goal is America and the west's
complete destruction)? Why does the greater body of Messiah
deftly remain silent while Jews are persecuted and even murdered
in Sweden, France, England, and Russia? Where's the outrage when
Muslim States continually deny Israel's right to exist? Where's the
outcry when Muslim terrorists use children and women as shields
in battle? Where was the rage and outcry when Hamas (Palestinian/
Arab Terrorist organization founded and funded by Iran) executed
hundreds of Palestine Liberation Organization (PLO) members
in front of their wives and families in Gaza in 2006 and 2007[5]?
Have we forgotten the brave and heroic men and woman of Ft.
Hood in 2009 that were murdered, wounded, and crippled at the
hands of an Islamic Terrorist? An Islamic Terrorist who wore the
uniform of a United States Army Officer! An enemy combatant
found wearing your Armed Forces uniforms is classified as a spy
by the Geneva Convention and should be dealt with accordingly!

What has happened to God's Commands in the Torah
given to us at Mt. Sinai; "Justice, only Justice you must pursue?"
Disobedience to God's word is a significant contributing factor in
America's decline and moral corruption! Ignorance, that's what I
refer to as the "dumbing down" of America. People won't protest
or fight something they know nothing about. People have become
apathetic; believing everything they hear from an extremely
biased and liberal press that unfairly reports biased information

against Israel. Scripture tells us to fight a good spiritual fight of righteousness and truth!

> *"Only conduct your lives in a way worthy of the Good News of the Messiah; so that whether I come and see you or I hear about you from a distance, you stand firm, united in spirit, fighting with one accord for the faith of the Good News, [28]not frightened by anything the opposition does. This will be for them an indication that they are headed for destruction and you for deliverance. And this is from God; [29]because for the Messiah's sake it has been granted to you not only to trust in him but also to suffer on his behalf, [30]to fight the same battles you once saw me fight and now hear that I am still fighting."* **Philippians 1:27-30**

Extremely few people are aware of the major spiritual crisis facing the Republic of America. Many citizens don't even know who their elected officials are and very few actually vote or get involved in politics! So many people can quote their favorite Hollywood Actor, Music Superstar, or who's winning a television reality show contest. They know what that person is wearing, they follow their blogs and twitter, they even know who is dating whom in Hollywood but remain clueless to the fact that their basic liberties and freedom are under attack and being taken away, bit by bit, every day. America is under siege from Islam and political correctness which hates purity, righteousness, and the Kingdom of God. The U.S. Treasury Department is seeking to become Shariah Law (Code of ethics based upon the Koran) compliant in its financial dealings with the Arab states which is unconstitutional[6]. I recently heard a well-known homosexual Hollywood actor share that he had two life missions; the Homosexual cause and separation of Church and State. The body of Messiah is society's moral conscience and all those who hate God and serve Satan seek the destruction of that conscience. Separation of Church and State policies coupled with political correctness are the tools of Satan who is plotting our destruction while most of America seems ignorant and apathetic. Soon it will be too late! Remember the words of Joseph Goebbels, the infamous Nazi Propagandist:

Tell a lie big enough and long enough and people will believe it!

Many of today's spiritual leaders possess a "Man Pleasing Spirit" that hinders the voice of truth.

> *"Now does that sound as if I were trying to win human approval? No! I want God's approval! Or that I'm trying to cater to people? If I were still doing that, I would not be a servant of the Messiah."* **Galatians 1:10**

Fear of God and obedience to His Mitzvahs and commands must be greater than the fear of any man, government, Islamic terrorist, or even death. Our leaders need a divine injection of biblical character, integrity, and honor. I appreciate all the Pastors and clergy who are serving God and tending His sheep in America. I thank God for their sacrifice and willingness to serve the King, but (I'm sorry to add this "but" to a compliment which I sincerely mean from the heart) don't fall into the trap of emotional, seeker sensitive ministry, coupled with some "feel good-you'll be O.K." sermons and Bible studies while failing to confront and tackle the actual complicated, political and moral issues America faces. The path of ignorance is all too convenient and easy for Spiritual leaders to follow; it's what the enemy desires. Over educated liberal clergy fail to lead their congregations in truth and action. They are often trained in universities and seminaries that refute the infallibility of God's written word. These clergy are likely to be politically correct, non-confrontational, seeker sensitive religious facades vice

God fearing men and woman like King David, King Jehu, or Paul. They pander to special interest groups and false religious beliefs that engage in and even espouse unbiblical behavior under the covering of "Grace".

> *"Proclaim the Word! Be on hand with it whether the time seems right or not. Convict, censure and exhort with unfailing patience and with teaching. ³For the time is coming when people will not have patience for sound teaching, but will cater to their passions and gather around themselves teachers who say whatever their ears itch to hear. ⁴Yes, they will stop listening to the truth, but will turn aside to follow myths. ⁵But you, remain steady in every situation, endure suffering, do the work that a proclaimer of the Good News should, and do everything your service to God requires."*
> **II Timothy 4:2-5**

The silence of our Christian and Godly Messianic Jewish leaders on a National Level (or in some cases their support of immoral, unbiblical special interest groups and even terrorist organizations such as Hamas and the PLO) strengthens the enemies' cause. Silence infers acceptance and compliance.

Remember, theology must conform too and reconcile with God's word. I'm sickened and disgusted by bible scholars, theologians, and pastors who teach, create, sign, and forward petitions to Americas governmental leaders seeking to divide the Land of Israel for an Arab state or espouse "Land for Peace" policies regarding Israel[7]. Remember the words of Yeshua (Yeshua is Jesus' actual name in Hebrew, what His mother called Him).

> *"You are salt for the Land. But if salt becomes tasteless, how can it be made salty again? It is no longer good for anything except being thrown out for people to trample on.*

¹⁴You are light for the world. A town built on a hill cannot be hidden. ¹⁵Likewise, when people light a lamp, they don't cover it with a bowl but put it on a lampstand, so that it shines for everyone in the house. ¹⁶In the same way, let your light shine before people, so that they may see the good things you do and praise your Father in heaven." **Matthew 5:13-16**

The Body of Messiah is to be the Moral conscience of the Republic, not a silent partner in support of sin, so start acting like talmidim (disciples) of Yeshua vice disciples of the world! You're not actively engaged in Kingdom work if some Pharisee somewhere isn't mad and upset with you! Let your LIGHT SHINE! Don't diffuse the light with false theology or political correctness! Be a voice of truth and do not remain silent.

"No one who has lit a lamp covers it with a bowl or puts it under a bed; no, he puts it on a stand; so that those coming in may see the light." **Luke 8:16**

Lack of unity among believers is also a problematic issue. Unity is mentioned throughout scripture but this biblical unity is with people of faith, followers of Yeshua! For clergy to seek unity with secularists, Muslims, or those who seek to divide Israel is unbiblical. Relationship is required but partnering isn't! God's formula for unity leads to Word Wide Revival.

"I united with them and you with me, so that they may be completely one, and the world thus realize that you sent me, and that you have loved them just as you have loved me." **John 17:23.**

Scriptural unity is between believing Jew (known as Messianic Jews) and believing Gentile. Not the Church and Islam, not the church and Orthodox Israel. We must be bold, we must be very bold and stand for biblical Kingdom truth and be vocal about it! Our actions must equal our words regarding God's absolute truth! Should you remain silent? History screams an emphatic and loud **NO**! Every follower of Yeshua must take action and unite Messianic Jew and believing Gentile, together as one and show our love for one another as God commands and change our world. But who are the Messianic Jews?

Chapter Two Notes

1. "*What if Jesus Had Never Been Born*" by Dr. D. James Kennedy and Jerry Newcombe:

2. Chisick, Harvey, "*Historical Dictionary of the Enlightenment*", Scarecrow Pr March 2005

3. Federer, William J. "*America's God and Country Encyclopedia of Quotations*" Amerisearch, INC 2000

4. Bullock, Alan, "*Hitler, A Study in Tyranny.*" New York, Harper & Row [©1962]

5. Mahnaimi, Uzi. Israel foils plot to kill Palestinian president, *The Sunday Times*, May 7, 2006

6. http://www.jewishworldreview.com/cols/gaffney110408.php3

7. United Nations Security Council Resolution 242

— Chapter 3 —

Messianic Israel

I. Who are the Messianic Jews?

Messianic Jews are Jews by birth and culture that have received and accepted Yeshua (Hebrew for Jesus) as their Messiah and substitute sin sacrifice. The term "Messianic" means having to do with the Messiah. Messianic Jews express their faith in a biblically prescribed fashion. Messianic Jews keep Shabbat (Friday at sunset until Saturday at sunset), celebrate the Biblical feasts, and believe and live both the Old and New Testament. The Messianic Jewish movement is an apostolic, prophetic, scriptural End Time movement. The Messianic movement is represented and expressed through numerous nationally recognized Jewish ministries such as Sid Roth's "Messianic Vision", Jonathan Bernis's "Jewish Voice", the M.J.A.A. (Messianic Jewish Alliance of America), the I.A.M.C.S (International Alliance of Messianic Congregations and Synagogues) and the U.M.J.C. (The Union of Messianic Jewish Congregations) to name a few.

God has birthed these organizations in an end time paradigm shift within the Christian community to teach the Body of Messiah how to be effective in sharing Yeshua with non Messianic Jews and to prepare the bride for the return of the Jewish Groom, Yeshua! A non-believing Jew is more likely to receive their Mashiach, the Jewish Messiah when Yeshua is presented within the correct biblical culture and context. Jews tend to reject the blue-eyed European Christian Jesus that persecuted and killed their families throughout history! The Messianic Jewish community is highly successful in sharing the Jewish Messiah with the Jewish people because they share the Gospel from the culturally correct and biblical context. The importance of Jewish salvations and Jewish revival will be shared in the next Chapter.

II. Is Yeshua (Jesus) a Jew and what does He want from me?

Yeshua was born a Jew in the land of Israel. He is the Son of God, born of a virgin through the Holy Spirit into this world 2,000 years ago. He was crucified, placed in a tomb for three days and three nights, and was resurrected from the dead on the third day. Yeshua will return in the near future to establish the Kingdom of God here on earth and rule from His throne in the Holy City of Jerusalem. Yeshua fulfilled over 50 Messianic Prophecies recorded throughout the Tanach (Old Testament). These are absolute truths, historical and biblical facts that cannot be denied or refuted.

Yeshua and his 12 talmidim (Hebrew for disciples) were Messianic Jews who believed in Yeshua's teachings and literally followed Yeshua wherever He went. They were taught and trained directly by Yeshua, spending 100% of their time with Him, immersed in Him. The talmidim then traveled throughout Israel and the known world after Yeshua's death and resurrection, teaching God's plan of Salvation through His son, Yeshua to the world, Jew and Gentile alike.

Yeshua desires that those who follow Him be His Ambassador, expanding the Kingdom of God here on earth. Ambassadorship requires us to truly know Yeshua, not the legend and the hype that religion has taught and espoused. Let's look at a few of the many aspects of who Yeshua really was and what He desires from you and the greater body of Messiah.

Yeshua called talmidim to "Come and Follow" Him now!

"Yeshua said to them, "Come after me, and I will make you fishers for men!" ²⁰At once they left their nets and went with him." **Matthew 4:19-20**

They followed Him immediately, not a day, week, or month later! God desires obedience and timeliness!

"When he had finished speaking, he said to Shim'on, 'Put out into deep water, and let down your nets for a catch.' ⁵Shim'on answered, 'We've worked hard all night long, Rabbi, and haven't caught a thing! But if you say so, I'll let down the nets.' ⁶They did this and took in so many fish that their nets began to tear. ⁷So they motioned to their partners in the other boat to come and help them; and they came and filled both boats to the point of sinking. ⁸When he saw this, Shim'on Kefa fell at Yeshua's knees and said, 'Get away from me, sir, because I'm a sinner!'" **Luke 5:4-11.**

Kefa (Peter) had just experienced a profound life changing epiphany. His act of obedience allowed God to open his eyes and heart concerning who was standing before him! Kefa falls to his knees before Yeshua, filled with divine revelation and states: "Get away from me, sir, because I'm a sinner!" He doesn't say Oh-it's the Mashiach, or Son of David, or "it's that carpenter guy from Nazareth! Kefa's spirit and soul recognize the Son of God in all of

His Glory and immediately there is conviction of his impurity and un-holiness, followed by astonishment:

> *"For astonishment had seized him and everyone with him at the catch of fish they had taken, and [10]likewise both Ya`akov and Yochanan, Shim`on's partners. 'Don't be frightened,' Yeshua said to Shim`on, 'from now on you will be catching men—alive!' [11]And as soon as they had beached their boats, they left everything behind and followed him."*
> **Luke 5:9-11**

Yeshua speaks to Kefa (Peter), Ya'akov (James), and Yochanan (John). "From now on you'll be catching men" and they beach their boats and immediately follow Him. Yeshua called them as well as us today to drop everything and follow Him, immediately. He wants you and I to be sold out to Him, completely. Yeshua does not want you postured with one foot in the world and one foot in the Kingdom. It's everything for the Kingdom and it's immediate. We dishonor God when we dawdle, when we drag our feet and dither in carrying out His instructions and commands. This reveals a life changing Kingdom truth, God doesn't "deal with you". I routinely hear this phrase in Christian conversations and circles: "Well, God is dealing with me about so and so or such and such..." God doesn't deal with you about anything. God is a King and His Kingdom is a Theocracy. The King issues decrees and orders. We, the loyal subjects are to be obedient and immediately carry out the Kings order or decree. God speaks, we do! It's that simple. As servants of the King our duty and responsibility is to be loyal and obedient subjects of His theocracy. Do not fall into the trap and snare of "Church Democracy" which is not biblical. The body of Messiah all too often attempts to cast votes regarding obedience to God's commands and decrees!

Through Peter's epiphany and obedience Yeshua gained the commitment of James and John! Don't keep your revelation and epiphany a secret! Your knowledge influences others! Each individual is responsible for cultivating a deeper foundation of understanding in order to be able to personally grow in the Kingdom and share the "Good News" with others.

> *"Everyone who comes to me, hears my words and acts on them—I will show you what he is like: ⁴⁸he is like someone building a house who dug deep and laid the foundation on bedrock. When a flood came, the torrent beat against that house but couldn't shake it, because it was constructed well. ⁴⁹And whoever hears my words but doesn't act on them is like someone who built his house on the ground without any foundation. As soon as the river struck it, it collapsed and that house became a horrendous wreck!"* **Luke 6:47-49**

Yeshua saw the hurting, rejected, sick, lame, and dying people around Him and was filled with Compassion.

> *"When he saw the crowds, he had compassion on them because they were harried and helpless, like sheep without a shepherd."* **Matthew 9:36**

Compassion is much harder than it seems. Compassion is being conscious of other people's distress combined with a desire to alleviate it. People have a tendency to associate with people like themselves which is Ok for recreation and fellowship but don't let walls of self righteousness separate you from the unsaved, hurt, lame, rejected, and broken people that surround you. Yeshua shared meals with tax collectors and prostitutes, he loved them! He had compassion for the sick and lame. Whenever I myself make a hospital visit I try to visit and pray with people in the hospital whom I don't know. We must get out of the "religious box" to share the "Good News"

Compassion requires you to quit thinking about self and take notice of the world around you. We are surrounded by suffering and broken people. The nation is at war, our service men are dying, military deployments are getting longer placing great stress on military families, the economy is bad, and people are losing their jobs and their homes. Corporations and Nations are going bankrupt. Bad economies cause people to increase their drug and alcohol abuse to ease the pain and suffering so addictions rise. The associated stress and depression also leads to higher suicide rates. When people ask me; "What can I do in the ministry?" My answer is: "Open your eyes and notice your surroundings and the people around you!" The world is hurting and waiting for Yeshua's ambassadors to intervene! We have the answers, we have the power and anointing Yeshua had, we have prayer, we have been given everything we need through Yeshua to impact our world for Him and remove the chains and shackles of oppression. Religion hates this because when you begin to act like Yeshua the oppressed are set free! We must remember Yeshua was a shepherd. What did Yeshua say to Peter after His resurrection?

> *"After breakfast Yeshua said to Simon Peter, 'Simon son of John, do you love me more than these?' 'Yes, Lord,' Peter replied, 'you know I love you.' 'Then feed my lambs,' Yeshua told him. [16]Yeshua repeated the question: 'Simon son of John, do you love me?' 'Yes, Lord,' Peter said, 'you know I love you.' 'Then take care of my sheep,' Yeshua said. [17]Once more he asked him, 'Simon son of John, do you love me?' Peter was grieved that Yeshua asked the question a third time. He said, 'Lord, you know everything. You know I love you.' Yeshua said, 'Then feed my sheep.'"* **John 21:15-17**

If you love Yeshua you'll take care of and tend His sheep! A Shepherd spends time among the sheep. He walks with them, he sleeps with them, he protects them from danger and when they're endangered he confronts that danger (David killed bears and lions before Goliath) and saves them. A shepherd provides for the needs of the flock. In the process of taking care of the sheep you acquire shepherd's robes. Shepherds robes are soiled and smell like sheep. Shepherds shoes are covered with sheep manure. Yeshua didn't walk around in a perfectly white, spotless robe looking down at the poor sheep, judging them, and being angry with them. In His compassion He went out among them and got soiled as He carried out His Father's wishes and tended the sheep. He had compassion for them, He healed them, He taught them, and He loved them! Are you filled with Yeshua's compassion? Go on, get out with the sheep and get dirty. It's what Yeshua would do!

Yeshua was also willing to intercede and get involved.

> *"Then a man afflicted with tzara`at came, kneeled down in front of him and said, 'Sir, if you are willing, you can make me clean.' ³Yeshua reached out his hand, touched him and said, 'I am willing! Be cleansed!' And at once he was cleansed from his tzara`at."* **Matthew 8:2-3**

The word "willing" used here means desire. It can read "Sir if you desire-and Yeshua answered I desire". Yeshua desired to help people. Desire means strong feelings coupled with a strong intention. Yeshua was willing to get involved. God wants to heal you; it's His desire, intention, aim, and want! He is willing. We have been given the same commission:

> *"Yes, indeed! I tell you that whoever trusts in me will also do the works I do! Indeed, he will do greater ones, because I am going to the Father."* **John 14:12**

Are your desires the same as Yeshua's? To be like Yeshua is to take your faith in Him and share it with the world, to the Jew first then also the nations.

Yeshua spent intimate time in the presence of His heavenly Father

"After he had sent the crowds away, he went up into the hills by himself to pray. Night came on, and he was there."
Matthew 14:23

Yeshua said He only did what He saw His Father in heaven do! This close intimacy with Father doesn't come from three to four minutes a day in prayer or praying only when there is a personal need or when you're in some sort of dire situation or trouble. You cannot hear the voice of the Lord and receive His direction if you're not spending intimate, quality time with Him!

Yeshua came for the lost sheep of Israel, He even wept over them!

"When Yeshua had come closer and could see the city, he wept over it, [42]saying, 'If you only knew today what is needed for shalom! But for now it is hidden from your sight.'"
Luke 19:41-42

Today, many who confess to following God have succumbed to the worlds view. Anti-Semitism in the world and Church today have risen to levels that matches or in some cases even exceeds that of pre-World War II Europe. The world seeks to divide and destroy Israel and Jerusalem instead of weeping over them. Over 90% of the Jewish people today are unsaved! The similar condition of Israel and the Jewish people 2,000 years ago pained Yeshua, He openly wept about it. Do you weep over the same issues and conditions that God and Yeshua do? Remember, Yeshua only did what He witnessed His Father in Heaven do. If Yeshua wept over Israel that means Father is weeping over Israel, what about you?

Sha'ul (Paul), whose ministry and calling was to the Gentile people knew and understood God's heart and confirmed his comprehension of it through the words he wrote. Sha'ul modeled Yeshua and set an example for us today when he stated that he would give up his own salvation if Israel could be saved.

> *"I am speaking the truth—as one who belongs to the Messiah, I do not lie; and also bearing witness is my conscience, governed by the Ruach HaKodesh: ²my grief is so great, the pain in my heart so constant, ³that I could wish myself actually under God's curse and separated from the Messiah, if it would help my brothers, my own flesh and blood."* **Romans 9:1-3**

Sha'ul (Paul) shared that the burden of his heart was the same burden as that of Yeshua's and God's heart!

> *"Brothers, my heart's deepest desire and my prayer to God for Isra'el is for their salvation."* **Romans 10:1**

This is a profound, heavenly revelation, a hidden mystery, Paul did what Jesus did! If the greater body of Messiah would grieve, weep, and pray over Israel and unsaved Jewish people the way God does we wouldn't be experiencing a dead church today. The body of Messiah must align itself with God's "heart's desire". The body should be weeping over the same things that God weeps over; it should grieve over the same things that grieve God. To be disciple of Yeshua means to act like Him. Yeshua told His followers to proclaim His salvation in the same manner and format that He did.

> *"And in his name repentance leading to forgiveness of sins is to be proclaimed to people from all nations, starting with Yerushalayim."* **Luke 24:47**

Every believer in the world has a call to bring the Good News to the world, to the Jew first!

> *"For I am not ashamed of the Good News, since it is God's powerful means of bringing salvation to everyone who keeps on trusting, to the Jew especially, but equally to the Gentile."* **Romans 1:16**

It's God's plan and His word! This is not something relegated to the Messianic Community only! There is a caution here; to follow God and be obedient you must be aware of this:

WARNING: FOLLOWING GOD'S PATTERN OF SHARING THE GOSPEL LEADS TO SUDDEN AND EXPLOSIVE KINGDOM GROWTH AND SPIRITUAL REVIVAL.

Quantum, Explosive Kingdom growth is the fruit God expects from us as His ambassadors before His Son returns for the bride.

III. What is a Talmidim (Disciple)?

A talmidim or Disciple is someone who follows the teachings and lifestyle of a certain teacher. A talmidim literally becomes like their master! To understand and comprehend Yeshua's Idioms, Parables, and Teachings it's imperative that we know Yeshua's cultural point of reference, setting, and context of who, where, and when He was teaching. Yeshua, the Jewish Messiah came for the lost House of Israel according to His own words

> *"He said, "I was sent only to the lost sheep of the house of Isra'el."* **Matthew 15:24**

Yeshua traveled throughout the Nation of Israel. He commissioned and trained twelve of His own people (Jews) to be

His talmidim or disciples. He celebrated and kept Shabbat (the biblical Sabbath, a day of rest and worship of God) and all the Biblical feasts in Jerusalem at the Temple or in a synagogue of whatever town He was currently in.

> "He taught in their synagogues, and everyone respected him. *16*Now when he went to Natzeret, where he had been brought up, on Shabbat he went to the synagogue as usual. He stood up to read, *17*and he was given the scroll of the prophet Yesha`yahu. Unrolling the scroll, he found the place where it was written, *18*The Spirit of ADONAI is upon me; therefore he has anointed me to announce Good News to the poor; he has sent me to proclaim freedom for the imprisoned and renewed sight for the blind, to release those who have been crushed, *19*to proclaim a year of the favor of ADONAI." *20*After closing the scroll and returning it to the shammash, he sat down; and the eyes of everyone in the synagogue were fixed on him. *21*He started to speak to them: 'Today, as you heard it read, this passage of the Tanakh was fulfilled!' *22*Everyone was speaking well of him and marvelling that such appealing words were coming from his mouth. They were even asking, 'Can this be Yosef's son?'" **Luke 4:15-22**

This scripture reveals Yeshua going to Synagogue on Shabbat "as usual", this was His culture and the setting for all of the New Testament (B'rit Hadasha in Hebrew). We see a biblically Jewish expression of faith practiced by Yeshua. Why is this important? Yeshua commands us to be his talmidim and go into the nations and make them talmidim, not believers, but talmidim.

> "Therefore, go and make people from all nations into talmidim, immersing them into the reality of the Father, the Son and the Ruach HaKodesh," **Matthew 28:19**

A talmidim literally becomes like their master! We are to be like Him and teach others to be like Him, to imitate Him! What did Yeshua do? He lived a First Century Jewish cultural and biblical lifestyle which included going to Synagogue, keeping Shabbat, and celebrating the feast days. This poses an interesting question. What do you mimic and who do you look like? Do you look like religion, Christianity, the world, or Yeshua?

IV. What did Yeshua do?

Yeshua never, I repeat, never once set foot in a Church because the Church didn't exist when He walked the earth. The Church wouldn't exist for another 300 plus years in the future. I know that statements like this ruffle religious feathers but we must fundamentally get back to absolute biblical truth in order to receive and walk in truth. Only the "Truth" will set us free! :

> *"All Scripture is God-breathed and is valuable for teaching the truth, convicting of sin, correcting faults and training in right living."* **II Timothy 3:16**

When this scripture was written The New Testament didn't exist. The scripture being referred to is the Tanach (Old Testament in Hebrew). The New Testament that you and I lovingly read and study from wouldn't exist for another 300 years in the future. The New Testament as we know it today was compiled in 367 A.D., 335 years after Yeshua was crucified[1]!

The B'rit Hadasha (New Testament) also reveals that God followed His biblical timeline and calendar, the Biblical feast days not the worlds.

> *"ADONAI said to Moshe, ²Tell the people of Isra'el: The designated times of ADONAI which you are to proclaim as holy convocations are my designated times."* **Leviticus 23:1-2**

"Designated times" in Hebrew is "Moedim", Divine Appointments. I like to think of it like this; God has designated specific times throughout the year through the annual feast day cycle in which He meets us! God has established Holy "Date Nights" with us! Holy Convocation in Hebrew means Holy Rehearsal. God uses the annual feast day cycle to teach us, the body of Messiah about the coming Kingdom that will be established here on Earth when Yeshua His Son returns. The feast days allows us to rehearse for that return, just like a wedding rehearsal. These days are called His Holy Days, not Jewish holidays. The scripture never refers to the Biblical feasts as "Jewish Holidays". God calls them appointed times (Moedim in Hebrew), His Holy days for all people to follow. The Biblical feasts are God's timeline!

Keeping the feasts of the Lord, God's appointed times places you in God's timeline versus man's. Why is this important? Following God's timeline prevents false theologies from confusing the body and drawing people away from God in apostasy. God operates according to His own calendar cycle and timeline. The Holy times, the feast days proclaim the seasons of rejoicing and repenting, fasting and feasting, keeping the Ke'hilot (Hebrew for congregation or assembly) pure!

The feasts are also the key to understanding God's eschatology. God can't take you farther than the Truth you believe. If we're truly going to break the mold of dying congregations and return to the power and Glory of God, the pattern must be right according to His timeline as recorded in His word.

There are seven Biblical feast days in the annual feast day cycle God commanded in Leviticus 23:

1) Shabbat.

"Work is to be done on six days; but the seventh day is a Shabbat of complete rest, a holy convocation; you are not to do any kind of work; it is a Shabbat for ADONAI, even in your homes." **Leviticus 23:3**

Shabbat, the seventh day of the week begins Friday at sunset and ends Saturday at sunset. Every day of the week is a recreation of the master's hand in creating the universe. Shabbat teaches the separation between the mundane and the Holy and represents God's covenant with us.

"God called the light Day, and the darkness he called Night. So there was evening, and there was morning, one day" **Genesis 1:5**

According to God's word the day begins at sunset in darkness. The Hebrew word for darkness: "Choshech" comes from the root word Chosh, which means something missing, unenergetic, lacking energy, powerless, aimless, hopeless, feared, suspected, worthless, and meaningless. Darkness or Choshech is comprised of all these descriptions! The enemy, HaSatan, the Devil, the Prince of Darkness is chosech or darkness.

The Hebrew word for Light is "Or" or ha Or which is the light! Or is the root word for illumination, joy, happiness, instruction, teaching, directive, order, woke up, roused, and parenthood. Yeshua is the light of the world! He is all of these descriptions!

Each and every day begins at sunset and is a recreation and teaching of God's creation of the universe. Each day begins just as the universe began in Choshech, powerless, beyond repair, aimless, hopeless, feared, suspected, secret, worthless, and meaningless. The day then streams towards the ha Or, the light. In creation God

Himself penetrated this hopelessness with His very being which is joy, happiness, instruction, teaching, directive, power, order, perfection, holiness, righteousness, purity, and love.

Shabbat is the culmination of this understanding, just as the day begins in chaos and streams towards the light; the week begins in such a manner and streams towards Shabbat. Shabbat separates the profane and mundane from the Holy! From this seven-day cycle we understand the seven millennial cycles of which the Kingdom of God is established in the beginning and streams towards the 7th millennium from creation when the Kingdom of Heaven will be here on Earth!

Shabbat is the holiest of the feast days as it was established in creation and there are 52 celebrations of it a year!

"God blessed the seventh day and separated it as holy; because on that day God rested from all his work which he had created, so that it itself could produce." **Genesis 2:3**

This scripture is the spiritual key to what makes Shabbat special: "God blessed the seventh day and separated it as holy". Shabbat is mentioned again in the Ten Commandments;

"Remember the day, Shabbat, to set it apart for God."
Exodus 20:8

Shabbat is a sign from God and the only commandment were are told to "remember":

"Tell the people of Isra'el, You are to observe my Shabbats; for this is a sign between me and you through all your generations; so that you will know that I am ADONAI, who sets you apart for me" **Exodus 31:13**

God reveals Himself through signs. Signs in Hebrew are "mofetim" which means extraordinary and surprising. Mofetim are signs employed by God to demonstrate His power and Will when He intervenes in the affairs of humanity. The rainbow is a sign, the ten plagues wrought against Egypt were signs, and the blood on the doorposts at Passover was a sign. A sign is a decree of God's presence. Signs represent the supernatural, the miraculous! Shabbat is a sign of creation; the master's hand at work here in the universe and in our daily lives!

2.) Passover.

3.) Feast of Unleavened Bread

These two feasts are celebrated together so I will discuss them together.

> *"These are the Lord's appointed feasts, the sacred assemblies you are to proclaim at their appointed times: ⁵The Lord's Passover begins at twilight on the fourteenth day of the first month. ⁶On the fifteenth day of that month the Lord's feast of Unleavened Bread begins; for seven days you must eat bread made without yeast. ⁷On the first day hold a sacred assembly and do no regular work. ⁸For seven days present an offering made to the Lord by fire. And on the seventh day hold a sacred assembly and do no regular work."*
> **Leviticus 23:4-8**

Passover begins just after the biblical calendar New Year.

> *"ADONAI spoke to Moshe and Aharon in the land of Egypt; he said, ²You are to begin your calendar with this month; it will be the first month of the year for you. ³Speak to all the assembly of Isra'el and say, On the tenth day of this*

month, each man is to take a lamb or kid for his family, one per household." **Exodus 12:1-3**

As the New Year begins, Passover is the first feast day celebrated as the annual cycle of Biblical feast celebrations is renewed. Commemorating the exodus from Egypt when the Angel of death passed over the first born of Israel, Passover is celebrated to teach the children the redemptive and salvation power of God. This celebration is actually two feast days; Passover and the Festival of Unleavened bread. The seven days of Matzah or unleavened bread reminds us of the quick exodus from Egypt when there was no time to bake bread with leavening.

The Passover Lamb sacrifice and the Matzah reveal the prophetic teaching and significance of Isaiah 53. Isaiah 53 gives the body signs and revelations concerning the Messiah who would be crucified as God's Passover Lamb. When Yeshua's blood is placed on the spiritual doorposts and lintels of your heart the angel of death will Passover you forever. Yeshua's last supper was actually the Passover Seder celebration. Yeshua also said He would celebrate this Seder again with His followers when He returned.

"For I tell you, it is certain that I will not celebrate it again until it is given its full meaning in the Kingdom of God." **Luke 22:16**

The importance of knowing and celebrating the feast days is significant as we celebrate them when Yeshua returns with Him! Israel also marked their entrance into the Promised Land by celebrating Passover:

"The people of Isra'el camped at Gilgal, and they observed Pesach on the fourteenth day of the month, there on the plains of Yericho. [11] The day after Pesach they ate what the

land produced, matzah and roasted ears of grain that day.
¹²The following day, after they had eaten food produced in the
land, the man (man is the Hebrew term for manna) ended.
From then on the people of Isra'el no longer had man; instead,
that year, they ate the produce of the land of Kena'an."
Joshua 5:10-12

Passover is the season of new beginnings, revival, and most
of all redemption! Pesach (Hebrew for Passover) celebrates our
salvation from slavery in Egypt and our salvation from the slavery
of sin through Yeshua and we will celebrate the Passover Seder with
Him when He returns!!

4.) Shavuot.

"Until the day after the seventh week; you are to count
fifty days; and then you are to present a new grain offering
to ADONAI. ¹⁷You must bring bread from your homes for
waving-two loaves made with one gallon of fine flour, baked
with leaven—as firstfruits for ADONAI". **Leviticus 23:16-17**

Shavuot means "weeks" in Hebrew, the Greek term is Pentecost.

Israel arrived at Mt. Sinai 50 days after the exodus from Egypt.
It was in Exodus chapters 19 & 20 that we hear the Shofar for
the first time and that the Torah was given to Moses and Israel in
chapter 20. This is the betrothal of Israel as the bride to God. The
basis for our wedding ceremonies comes from this God encounter.
The sages teach that at Mount Sinai God reached out from heaven
and kissed the face of Israel, His bride. Then, 2,000 years ago we
received a supernatural and spectacular gift from heaven on this
exact same day.

"The festival of Shavu'ot arrived, and the believers all
gathered together in one place. ²Suddenly there came a sound

from the sky like the roar of a violent wind, and it filled the whole house where they were sitting. ³Then they saw what looked like tongues of fire, which separated and came to rest on each one of them. ⁴They were all filled with the Ruach HaKodesh and began to talk in different languages, as the Spirit enabled them to speak." **Acts 2:1-4**

On the same feast day that Israel received the Torah, God poured out His Ruach Hakodesh (Holy Spirit in Hebrew). The 120 people in that upper room who received the outpouring of the Holy Spirit were Messianic Jews who were in Jerusalem for the biblical feast of Shavuot or Pentecost. These Jewish talmidim of Yeshua would go into the world and lead a majority of that known world to faith in the Jewish Messiah. As Jewish believers in Yeshua they transformed the gentile nations using only the Tanach (Old Testament) and the infilling of the Ruach HaKodesh which is the Holy Spirit in Hebrew. What a testimony and example they gave us 2,000 years ago!

5.) Yom Teruah (Feast of Trumpets)

6.) Yom Kippur (Day of Atonement or more accurately Day of Purging).

I want to speak about these two feasts together for they have not yet been spiritually fulfilled. God has fulfilled the prophetic destiny of the other feast days through His Son Yeshua and through the Holy Spirit. These two feast days have not yet been prophetically fulfilled:

"ADONAI said to Moshe, ²⁴Tell the people of Isra'el, In the seventh month, the first of the month is to be for you a day of complete rest for remembering, a holy convocation announced with blasts on the shofar. ²⁵Do not do any kind

of ordinary work, and bring an offering made by fire to ADONAI. ²⁶*ADONAI said to Moshe,* ²⁷*The tenth day of this seventh month is Yom-Kippur; you are to have a holy convocation, you are to deny yourselves, and you are to bring an offering made by fire to ADONAI.* ²⁸*You are not to do any kind of work on that day, because it is Yom-Kippur, to make atonement for you before ADONAI your God.* ²⁹*Anyone who does not deny himself on that day is to be cut off from his people;* ³⁰*and anyone who does any kind of work on that day, I will destroy from among his people.* ³¹*You are not to do any kind of work; it is a permanent regulation through all your generations, no matter where you live.* ³²*It will be for you a Shabbat of complete rest, and you are to deny yourselves; you are to rest on your Shabbat from evening the ninth day of the month until the following evening."* **Leviticus 23:23:32**

Leviticus 23 tells us that the blowing of the Shofar is a memorial but not to what! Yom Terua, the day of the Shofar, is, I believe, the day of Messiah's returns to Judge and determine whose name stays in or is blotted out of the book of life. First, Yeshua returns at the sounding of the Shofar!

"Then the Son of Man will appear in the sky, all tribes of the land will mourn, and they will see the Son of Man coming in the clouds of heaven with tremendous power and glory. ³¹*He will send out His angels with a Great Shofar; and they will gather together His chosen people from the four winds, from one ends of heaven to the other."* **Matthew 24:30-31**

Yom Teru'ah is thus a day of crying out to God, to remind Him that we are His people. It is the day that we rehearse and celebrate the return of Messiah as we look towards the glorious wedding feast celebration!

The 10-day period between Yom Teruah and Yom Kippur is known as the "10 Days of Awe". It is a time of deep personal reflection, a time of soul searching and repentance. During this time frame there is a phrase said between the Jewish people "May your name remain in the Book of Life". Yeshua returns at the heavenly sounding of the Shofar as rehearse on Yom Teruah to Judge the World.

> *"When the Son of Man comes in his glory, accompanied by all the angels, he will sit on his glorious throne. ³²All the nations will be assembled before him, and he will separate people one from another as a shepherd separates sheep from goats. ³³The `sheep' he will place at his right hand and the `goats' at his left"* **Matthew 25:31-33**

The end of the 10 Days of Awe is marked by Yom Kippur. Yom Kippur is the only time of the year that the High Priest actually entered into the Holy of Holies. Yom means "day" in Hebrew and Kippur is translated as Atonement but this is not accurate. Kippur actually means, "purge" in Hebrew.

Yeshua returns at the sounding of the Shofar. During the Ten Days of Awe He is judging the Nations. Sheep, who are obedient and listen to the voice of the Shepherd, go the right side of Yeshua! The side of salvation! Goats, which are rebellious and won't listen to the voice of the Shepherd, go to His left, the side of wrath and hell. This judgment period culminates with Yom Kippur (Day of Purging) when those who go to the left have their name "blotted out" or "purged" from the "Book of Life" contrary to popular theology, scripture states that your name is recorded in the "Book of Life" when you're born.

"Your eyes could see me as an embryo, but in your book all my days were already written; my days had been shaped before any of them existed." **Psalms 139:16**

How you live your life judged against the word of God determines if your name will remain in the book or be blotted out!

"He who wins the victory will, like them, be dressed in white clothing; and I will not blot his name out of the Book of Life; in fact, I will acknowledge him individually before my Father and before his angels." **Revelation 3:5**

Those who are on the right side of Yeshua will go to the Wedding feast represented by Sukkot or Feast of Tabernacles.

7.) Sukkot

"ADONAI said to Moshe, ³⁴Tell the people of Isra'el, On the fifteenth day of this seventh month is the feast of Sukkot for seven days to ADONAI. ³⁵On the first day there is to be a holy convocation; do not do any kind of ordinary work. ³⁶For seven days you are to bring an offering made by fire to ADONAI; on the eighth day you are to have a holy convocation and bring an offering made by fire to ADONAI; it is a day of public assembly; do not do any kind of ordinary work." **Leviticus 23:33-36**

Sukkot or Feast of Tabernacles is celebrated as the feast of the Lord that commemorates God's provision to Israel as they wandered in the wilderness for forty years after the Exodus from Egypt. Jewish people build small temporary structures called "sukkah's" outside their homes and stay in them during the length of this feast day. The sukkah looks amazingly like the wedding "chuppah" (canopy) used in Jewish weddings. The sukkah is a prophetic portrait of the bridal chamber that we will share with our Groom, Yeshua when He returns.

"Finally, everyone remaining from all the nations that came to attack Yerushalayim will go up every year to worship the king, ADONAI-Tzva'ot, and to keep the festival of Sukkot. ¹⁷If any of the families of the earth does not go up to Yerushalayim to worship the king, ADONAI-Tzva'ot, no rain will fall on them." **Zechariah 14:16-17**

V. When was Yeshua Born?

It is a common misconception and a common phrase I often hear; "No one actually knows when Yeshua was born". This is untrue and I will show you why. Yeshua was born during the Feast of Passover! Exactly six months after Yochanan's (John the Baptist) conception, Yeshua was conceived by the Ruach HaKodesh.

"In the days of Herod, King of Y'hudah, there was a cohen named Z'kharyah who belonged to the Aviyah division. His wife was a descendant of Aharon, and her name was Elisheva. ⁶Both of them were righteous before God, observing all the mitzvot and ordinances of Adonai blamelessly. ⁷But they had no children, because Elisheva was barren; and they were both well along in years." **Luke 1:5-6**

"When his period of his Temple service was over he returned home. ²⁴Following this, Elisheva his wife conceived, and she remained five months in seclusion, saying, ²⁵Adonai has done this for me; he has shown me favor at this time, so as to remove my public disgrace. ²⁶In the sixth month, the angel Gavri'el was sent by God to a city in the Galil called Natzeret, ²⁷to a virgin engaged to a man named Yosef, of the house of David; the virgin's name was Miryam. ²⁸Approaching her, the angel said, "Shalom", favored lady! Adonai is with you! ²⁹She was deeply troubled by his words and wondered what kind of greeting this might be. ³⁰The angel said to her, Don't

be afraid, Miryam, for you have found favor with God.
[31]Look! You will become pregnant, you will give birth to a
son, and you are to name him Yeshua. [32]He will be great,
he will be called Son of HaElyon. Adonai, God, will give
him the throne of his forefather David; [33]and he will rule
the House of Ya'akov forever—there will be no end to his
Kingdom." **Luke 1:23-33**

The key here is the duty cycle of Z'kharyah. Temple records record the Aviyah division working their priestly duties at the Temple in what would equate to the month of January in the western calendar. That means when Z'kharyah returned home to Elisheva, they conceived Yochanan. Pregnant for nine months, Yochanan was born in the fall month of October according to the Gregorian calendar, the seventh biblical month. Scripture records that six months after Yochanan was born, Yeshua was born which places Yeshua's birth on the 1st day of the first month (1st of Nisan) of the biblical New year of 6 B.C. Spring is when God orders that we start our calendars in the biblical month of Nissan when we celebrate Passover (Pesach).

"You are to begin your calendar with this month; it
will be the first month of the year for you. [3]Speak to all the
assembly of Isra'el and say, On the tenth day of this month,
each man is to take a lamb or kid for his family, one per
household." **Exodus 12:2-3**

The 1st day of the first month is when the annual feast day cycle is renewed and begins the New Year. Our "New Beginning", Yeshua was born on the first day of the Biblical New Year.

I have just presented a basic review of the feast day cycle and the prophetic outline of their eschatological importance. This was in no manner meant to be an exhaustive or comprehensive feast day study. I preferred instead to give a quick, informal explanation. I pray this reveals how God follows His own feast day cycle and how Yeshua has and will fulfill their prophetic purpose.

God follows His own timeline not a man-made timeline. It begins when His Son, Yeshua, was born in the First Day of the New Year, He celebrated the Passover Seder with His talmidim, He was crucified and Resurrected during Passover, and according to the book of Matthew returns on the sounding of the Shofar (Yom Teruah) to Judge the world (Yom Teruah-Day of Atonement)!

What did Yeshua do? He lived a culturally and biblical First Century Jewish life! He taught in Jewish Synagogues, kept Shabbat as was His habit and He celebrated all the Biblical feasts. A friend once told me: "the closer a person gets to God, the more Jewish they look" How true!

V. Why aren't Messianic Jews just called Christian or Christian Jews?

Christ is the Greek term for the Hebrew word Mashiach which means, "anointed one". Jesus is the English nickname for Yeshua which means salvation in Hebrew. Yeshua is the real name given to Jesus by His mother and father at birth. Knowing the correct context and cultural importance of His name, Yeshua is what He should be called. It's not a salvation issue but it is a love issue of respect, honor, and humility. Scripture records the profound impact of His birth name.

"Therefore God raised him to the highest place and gave him the name above every name; [10]that in honor of the name given Yeshua, every knee will bow—in heaven, on earth and under the earth" **Philippians 2:9-10**

Church, Christian, Christians, or Christianity (Greco/Roman terms for gentile followers of the Way) are all terms rarely used in the Messianic community. Why? History records over 2,000 years of persecution and murders. When all are combined together tens of millions of Jews have been killed at the hands of Christians through the Inquisition, Crusades, Pogroms (Jewish Persecution in Russia), and the Holocaust simply because they were Jews. This dark and violent history has fostered a great distrust of Christians within the Jewish community because of their Anti-Semitic behavior throughout history. If you're a God fearing, Spirit filled Christian who loves Israel and the Jewish people please cleanse your terminology of Christian slang. It opens doors for you to share the Jewish Messiah with the Jewish people. The greatest act of love you could show a Jewish person is to share their Jewish Messiah with them! If you live and act like Yeshua you will be a magnet for unsaved Jewish people. A Messianic Israel is the key for the return of Yeshua, the Jewish Messiah!

Chapter Three Notes

1. Gamble, Harry Y.: "*The New Testament Canon: Its Making and Meaning*". Philadelphia: Fortress, 1985.

— Chapter 4 —

The First Body

I. Who were the first believers?

This is critical information to the greater body of Messiah today! Scripture records that the first body of believers raised the dead, healed the sick, were translated across great geographical distances and daily walked in the power and anointing of God. They set the foundation, the metric for what the body should be like today so that we too may walk in the same way! So who were they? They were cultural Jews, talmidim of Yeshua, and Messianic Jews. They followed Yeshua's teachings, commands, and culture as they seeded and birthed Messianic Congregations throughout the known world ruled by the Roman Empire. Remember, the Church as its' known today wouldn't exist for another 300 plus years in the future. Their numbers grew daily as scripture records their pattern of ministry.

> *"For I am not ashamed of the Good News, for it is the power of God to salvation for everyone who believes, for the Jew first and also for the Greek"* **Romans 1:16**

The Author of this scripture, Sha'ul or Paul (his Greek name) was a Jew from the tribe of Benjamin. His heart and attitude regarding Israel was revealed in Romans 9.

"In the presence of Messiah, I speak with utter truthfulness—I do not lie—and my conscience and the Holy Spirit confirm that what I am saying is true. ²My heart is filled with bitter sorrow and unending grief ³for my people, my Jewish brothers and sisters. I would be willing to be forever cursed—cut off from Messiah—if that would save them. ⁴They are the people of Israel, chosen to be God's special children. God revealed his glory to them. He made covenants with them and gave his law to them. They have the privilege of worshiping him and receiving his wonderful promises. ⁵Their ancestors were great people of God, and Christ himself was a Jew as far as his human nature is concerned. And he is God, who rules over everything and is worthy of eternal praise! Amen" **Romans 9:1-5**

Paul was willing to give up his own salvation if Israel might be saved! This concept has been lost within the Church over the last millennia. I myself, as a Jewish believer, have a Mezuzah nailed to the doorpost of my homes front door. On the front doorpost of every Jewish home is such a Mezuzah which is a small cylindrical device, 4-5 inches long and about one half an inch wide made from a variety of materials that can withstand outdoor elements. Encased inside the Mezuzah is a small parchment with the following biblical passages;

(A typical Mezuzah)

"Sh'ma, Yisra'el! ADONAI Eloheinu, ADONAI echad [Hear, Isra'el! ADONAI our God, ADONAI is one]; ⁵and you are to love ADONAI your God with all your heart, all your being and all your resources. ⁶These words, which I am

*ordering you today, are to be on your heart; ⁷and you are to
teach them carefully to your children. You are to talk about
them when you sit at home, when you are traveling on the
road, when you lie down and when you get up. ⁸tie them
on your hand as a sign, put them at the front of a headband
around your forehead"* **Deuteronomy 6:4-9**

The Mezuzah is a device used to fulfill God's command to
mark and identify the doorposts of your home with His word!
Every believer in Yeshua should consider hanging a Mezuzah on
their front door post. It is a visible proclamation and testimony
of the "Living Word" who is Yeshua and lets the world know that
your home is covered by the Word of God just as He commanded!

The point of my digression here is that when various Christian
missionaries knock on my door and I don't have the time to talk
with them (I actually love to invite them into my home and talk
with them about the absolute truth of God's word but I don't
always have the time!) I just point to the Mezuzah nailed to my
front doorpost and tell them "I'm Jewish". Without exception,
every one of those missionaries to date have apologized, turned
and walked away from my home. What a great tragedy! Instead
of being the first ministered to it seems we are always the last!
Romans 1:16 states specifically that they should be sharing the
Gospel to the **Jews first** yet they all turn and walk away!

Not sharing the Gospel with Jewish people is the plan of
Satan. Yeshua, the First Messianic Jew and Son of God brought
salvation to the world!

*"You people don't know what you are worshipping; we
worship what we do know, because salvation comes from the
Jews"* **John 4:22**

The "Good News" of this salvation was then taken by those Jewish talmidim into the world. If you are a follower of Yeshua today it's because a faithful, spirit filled Messianic Jew took the Gospel message to the nation's 1,950 years ago. Got Salvation? Thank a Jew!

III. Spiritual Revelation.

"The following day Moshe sat to settle disputes for the people, while the people stood around Moshe from morning till evening. [14]When Moshe's father-in-law saw all that he was doing to the people, he said, "What is this that you are doing to the people? Why do you sit there alone, with all the people standing around you from morning till evening?"
Exodus 18:13-14

"But you should choose from among all the people competent men who are God-fearing, honest and incorruptible to be their leaders, in charge of thousands, hundreds, fifties and tens. [22]Normally, they will settle the people's disputes. They should bring you the difficult cases; but ordinary matters they should decide themselves. In this way, they will make it easier for you and share the load with you. [23]If you do this—and God is directing you to do it—you will be able to endure; and all these people too will arrive at their destination peacefully."
Exodus 18:21-23

What's the purpose of Yitro's (Jethro in English) visit to Moses just before Israel arrives at Mt. Sinai? Yitro is Moses' father-in-law and Moses' teacher in desert survival. There were several critical areas of learning Moses needed in order to lead the fledgling nation of Israel. The first part of Moses learning was statesmanship, international diplomacy, and principles of governing he received as a prince of Egypt. Moses second phase of learning from Yitro were the survival skills required to lead Israel in the desert wilderness, live off of the land, find water, and tend flocks.

Yitro observes Moses attempting to perform all these tasks by himself. Moses has no time left for God or his family. Yitro knows Moses desperately needs help or he'll lose everything. The timing of this visit is critical because God can't instill heavenly revelation into Moses and the Israelites while Moses is consumed with the daily bureaucratic, inter-tribal, inter-personal, disputes and rulings that completely consume his time.

If Satan can't tempt you in sin, he'll get you busy! Moses is the only figure in the bible to have received profound, brand new revelation directly from heaven. All the other Prophets and even Yeshua teach from and comment on the first five books of the bible, the Torah. Moses received the first five books (called the Torah), the word of God directly from heaven! Yitro taught Moses the art of delegation which provided the relief Moses needed to receive God's divine revelation.

This same tactic is used today by Satan. Busyness is a major reason why the church today is not hearing God's Divine revelation. Currently, in our day there is a radical, spiritual paradigm shift occurring within the body of Messiah. There is a fresh stream of God's presence being poured out from heaven, right now. This stream is as old as the ancient of days. God spoke of it in the beginning of time yet it's just now being poured out in our day. So many believers today are like Moses, their time is consumed with church programs, services, and works. They're too busy to recognize and receive Gods fresh revelation from heaven. Instead, they are consumed with this church busyness leaving little or no time for God and family! Don't get bogged down with busyness and miss God!

Scripture clearly reveals God's heart and mind regarding this fresh outpouring. This shift is a major movement within the greater body of Messiah that is restoring unity between Messianic Jew and Gentile Christians! The overall body hasn't experienced it or seen it yet because they're too busy and not looking for it. A great awakening is unfolding right now as God is stirring our awareness.

IV. Reticular Activation System.

The Reticular Activating System (RAS) is a part of the brain connected to the brain stem that is responsible for behavioral alertness; it's the attention center of the brain[1]. It enables the brain to process and learn new information. Let me give an example. Imagine that you walk into your favorite lawn and garden store. As you enter into the store you immediately see a myriad of sale signs. Think of the entire stimulus your brain is receiving. There is the background noise within the store of people talking, light music, announcements for customer assistance etc. How much of this information does your mind actually process and bring to your cognitive attention? Almost none but why? Because all of this background information is irrelevant to what you're looking for. Yes you hear the general background noise and see all the products and signs but they're not brought to the fore front of your thoughts and mind because it's not relevant to your purpose for being there, it's not related to what you are looking for.

Let's say your purpose for going to the store today was to purchase a new gas grill because yours rusted through last winter. You're walking towards the section of the store that sells the gas grilles when a see a sign saying "ALL GAS GRILL PRICES ARE REDUCED 50%." Suddenly your attention level has peaked. Your Reticular Activating System, that mechanism inside your brain that flushes pertinent and relevant information you're looking for to your full attention. Bells and whistles go off in your head because of your RAS! Here is the irony, that sign has probably been there for months and the last 5 times you visited that store you walked right past the same exact sign but you ignored it because the previous 5 times you were there you weren't looking for "Gas Grills". Your reticular activating system (RAS) didn't process the sign and you walked right past it without a glance. It was critical information but you ignored it previously because you weren't looking for it.

Let's look at this event with Yitro and Moshe again but this time with your Reticular System activated, looking for unity. Just prior to Yitro's words of wisdom to Moses, God had delivered Israel from slavery in Egypt through ten plagues. This revelation of God's power and might caused something extraordinary to happen when Israel departed Egypt:

> "The people of Isra'el traveled from Ra'amses to Sukkot, some six hundred thousand men on foot, not counting children. 38A mixed crowd also went up with them, as well as livestock in large numbers, both flocks and herds"
> **Exodus 12:37-38**

Two small words "Mixed Crowd" reveal a piece of critical information that few have paid attention to throughout history because they weren't looking for it, their RAS wasn't activated.

The 70 descendants of Jacob who entered into Israel had now grown into millions. God's signs and wonders were seen and felt by Israel, the Egyptians, and every people group in the land at that time! Egypt, the world's only super power at the time also had the world's best universities and libraries. In Egypt, as the plagues were being wrought, there were students, scholars and learned men of the world's nations studying, teaching, and being educated in these world class institutions of higher learning. Egypt also had Nubian and other Semite slaves beside those of Israel. God was not only revealing Himself to Israel and Egypt through those ten plagues, but to the nations of the world. Those who had their RAS activated knew the truth when they saw, heard, and experienced God. Individuals and families from every one of these people groups departed Egypt along with Israel. This now explains what happened at Mt. Sinai when God spoke directly to Israel for the first time. Remember, for over 200 years of slavery Israel cried out to God for redemption but God never answers them or talks to them directly until Mt Sinai. Until then, God had only spoken to Moses and Aaron.

"On the morning of the third day, there was thunder, lightning and a thick cloud on the mountain." **Exodus 19:16**

Thunder in Hebrew is "kolot" This literally means a "multitude of voices". I want you to understand that the Mt Sinai event is occurring on the festival of Shavuot (Pentecost). It's happening 50 days after Israel's departure from Egypt. The day the Torah was given, the first five books of the bible is also the same exact day some 1,700 years later that the Holy Spirit is given in the upper room in Jerusalem after Yeshua's resurrection.

Kolot, the "multitude of voices" was spoken by God so the "mixed Crowd" comprised of the world's cultures and languages could hear the voice of God and His instructions. This mixed crowd that left Egypt with Israel were from Africa, the Middle East, Asia Minor, the Orient, India, and what we know of today as Europe heard God's voice and commands. All seventy known root languages were coming from the top of the mountain conveying Gods instructions for ALL HUMANITY! We just haven't observed this in the past because our RAS hadn't been activated. We also experience a similar event from the New Testament.

> *"The festival of Shavu'ot arrived, and the believers all gathered together in one place. ²Suddenly there came a sound from the sky like the roar of a violent wind, and it filled the whole house where they were sitting. ³Then they saw what looked like tongues of fire, which separated and came to rest on each one of them. ⁴They were all filled with the Ruach HaKodesh and began to talk in different languages, as the Spirit enabled them to speak."* **Acts 2:1-4**

Roar in the Greek is "fer'-o" which means to bring forth, produce; to bring forward in a speech. The Word of God was once again was going forth in the multitude of voices "kolot" as those Jewish men and women in that upper room talked in different languages so the Mixed Crowds heard God's voice. Both events happened on the same exact date and celebration, just different millennia.

The miracles at Mt Sinai and that upper room experience weren't immediately understood or comprehended. Peter was given a dream in Acts 10 so the talmidim would come to realize and understand what God had just done. Peter recounts the dream and its meaning in Acts chapter eleven. Let's walk this through verse by verse.

> *"The emissaries and the brothers throughout Y'hudah heard that the Goyim had received the word of God."* **Acts 11:1**

This wasn't the first time. Remember, the Goyim heard God's voice at Mt. Sinai but it hadn't been noticed by the Talmidim because their RAS wasn't energized, they weren't looking for it.

For the talmidim this was a radical paradigm shift that was almost outside their ability to comprehend. Two thousand years ago Gentiles were considered unholy and impure by Israelites. Jews in Yeshua's day did not associate whatsoever with Gentiles. Gentiles were considered unclean. The report that Gentiles were receiving God was almost unbelievable!

> *"But when Kefa went up to Yerushalayim, the members of the Circumcision faction criticized him, [3]saying, "You went into the homes of uncircumcised men and even ate with them!"* **Acts 11:2-3**

Peter (Kefa) actually went into a Gentiles home and broke bread with them! The Messianic Community didn't understand what was happening. It's human nature to persecute and destroy what's not understood. Ironically, the reverse is happening today as Jewish people are coming to faith. Many in the church criticize Messianic Jews with their biblical customs in their midst

> *"In reply, Kefa began explaining in detail what had actually happened: [5]I was in the city of Yafo, praying; and in a trance I had a vision. I saw something like a large sheet being lowered by its four corners from heaven, and it came down to me. [6]I looked inside and saw four-footed animals, beasts of prey, crawling creatures and wild birds. [7]Then I heard a voice telling me, 'Get up, Kefa, slaughter and eat!' [8]I said, 'No, sir! Absolutely not! Nothing unclean or treif has ever entered my mouth!' [9]But the voice spoke again from heaven: 'Stop treating as unclean what God has made clean.' [10]This happened three times, and then everything was pulled back up into heaven. [11]At that very moment, three men who had been sent to me from Caesarea arrived at the house where I was staying; [12]and the Spirit told me to have no misgivings about going back with them. These six brothers also came*

with me, and we went into the man's house. ¹³He told us how he had seen the angel standing in his house and saying, 'Send to Yafo and bring back Shim'on, known as Kefa. ¹⁴He has a message for you which will enable you and your whole household to be saved.' ¹⁵But I had hardly begun speaking when the Ruach HaKodesh fell on them, just as on us at the beginning! ¹⁶And I remembered that the Lord had said, 'Yochanan used to immerse people in water, but you will be immersed in the Ruach HaKodesh.' ¹⁷Therefore, if God gave them the same gift as he gave us after we had come to put our trust in the Lord Yeshua the Messiah, who was I to stand in God's way? ¹⁸On hearing these things, they stopped objecting and began to praise God, saying, "This means that God has enabled the Goyim as well to do t'shuvah and have life!"
Acts 11:4-18

Peter (Kefa) was receiving MIND BENDING and NUMBING revelation two thousand years ago. The Gentiles receiving the Ruach HaKodesh (Holy Spirit) was so radically outside the talmidim's (disciples) realm of understanding and teaching that God had to single out Kefa, who also didn't understand, and gave him a supernatural dream and vision so he would understand. The dream was confirmed by the Gentiles knocking at his door to take him to Caesarea as God had revealed. I can't say this enough; the theology of two thousand years ago could not comprehend Gentiles following the God of Israel or Gentiles being filled with the Holy Spirit! This dream was prophetic and not about food! In the same way, today's man made theology can't seem to comprehend Jews receiving their Messiah Yeshua and being filled once again with the Ruach HaKodesh! Upon his arrival in Caesarea, Kefa shares with Cornelius and the others there his revelation.

> *"Then Kefa addressed them: I now understand that God does not play favorites, [35] but that whoever fears him and does what is right is acceptable to him, no matter what people he belongs to."* **Acts 10:34-35**

Peter also shared the revelation with the other talmidim because Paul (Sha'ul in Hebrew), whose ministry was to the Gentiles, wrote extensively about this!

> *"That means that there is no difference between Jew and Gentile—ADONAI is the same for everyone, rich toward everyone who calls on him"* **Romans 10:12**

God is restoring the Messianic Jew back into the mainstream body of Messiah after almost 1,800 years. Many believers don't comprehend because of their doctrine and theology but like 2,000 years ago, it will happen regardless. The greater body of Messiah has been asleep for a long time. God is restoring His covenant people back into the body of Messiah and fulfilling His plans to establish His Kingdom here on the Earth.

V. Why does God keep Israel and the Messianic Jew?

God has kept Israel and the Messianic Jew because He is a covenant God. He never goes back on His own word; in fact God states His word shall be accomplished:

> *"So is my word that goes out from my mouth—it will not return to me unfulfilled; but it will accomplish what I intend, and cause to succeed what I sent it to do."* **Isaiah 55:10**

God's word is specific and does not return void. He keeps His word forever. The Land of Israel belongs to the nation of Israel.

God is not done with the Jewish people. The following scriptures confirm this:

> *"He remembers his covenant forever, the word he commanded to a thousand generations, ⁹the covenant he made with Avraham, the oath he swore to Yitz'chak, ¹⁰and established as a law for Ya'akov, for Isra'el as an everlasting covenant: ¹¹To you I will give the land of Kena'an as your allotted heritage."* **Psalms 105:8-11**

> *"In that case, I say, isn't it that God has repudiated his people?" Heaven forbid! For I myself am a son of Isra'el, from the seed of Avraham, of the tribe of Binyamin. ²God has not repudiated his people, whom he chose in advance. Or don't you know what the Tanakh says about Eliyahu? He pleads with God against Isra'el."* **Romans 11:1-2**

These passages provide a firm biblical foundation and reveal the absolute truth of God's word. **GOD IS NOT DONE WITH ISRAEL OR HIS PEOPLE,** the Jewish people. Paul said:

> *"For God's free gifts and his calling are irrevocable."* **Romans 11:29**

God chose Israel and their biblical culture to be His voice piece, to share Himself with the world, to be the world's evangelists.

> *"He has said, 'It is not enough that you are merely my servant to raise up the tribes of Ya'akov and restore the offspring of Isra'el. I will also make you a light to the nations, so my salvation can spread to the ends of the earth."* **Isaiah 49:6**

Israel is the land, culture, and people into which God brought forth His only Son. Yeshua will return to the same land, people, and culture in the very near future.

VI. What is Israel's purpose in Yeshua's Return?

As spoken through the prophets and their writings, Israel's heavenly calling and destiny is to be a light unto the world. That calling is irrevocable according to Romans 11:29. This calling upon Israel is directly connected to Yeshua's words spoken over Israel 2,000 years ago.

> *"Yerushalayim! Yerushalayim! You kill the prophets! You stone those who are sent to you! How often I wanted to gather your children, just as a hen gathers her chickens under her wings, but you refused!* [38]*Look! God is abandoning your house to you, leaving it desolate.* [39]*For I tell you, from now on, you will not see me again until you say, `Blessed is he who comes in the name of ADONAI.'"* **Matthew 23:37-39**

Yeshua's words reveal the global necessity for revival among the Jewish people. Yeshua will not return and establish God's Kingdom here on earth until Israel cries out "Baruch H'Ba B'Shem Adonai" which is Hebrew for "Blessed is he who comes in the name of the Lord".

Israel, in the near future, will become Messianic. Israel and the Jewish people will openly receive Yeshua as their Savior and King as a nation. Israel will collectively mourn the "lost son of the house of Israel" (Zechariah 12:10) and as a nation they will call on Yeshua to return as their King to Rule over Israel and the world from Jerusalem. This global Kingdom event occurs only when *Israel* cries out "Blessed is He who comes in the Name of the Lord"!

I know this destroys a few religious idols and golden calves of eschatology and theology. The words are from the Master Himself, they are not mine! Man-made eschatology and theology does not trump the words of Yeshua. Theology and eschatology must reconcile to scripture. All doctrine and teaching must concur with and reconcile to God's written word or its heresy. Be extremely cautious of partially quoted scriptures, scripture quoted out of context, and teachings that are contrary to or dispute Yeshua's own words, it's not truth!

VII. Replacement Theology.

Why hasn't the body of Messiah experienced or witnessed Jewish revival? Why isn't Israel saved and calling upon Yeshua to return and reign as our King? Israel hasn't received Yeshua yet because a hideous plan from hell has hindered Jewish evangelism. A plan that's incredibly simple and yet in plain view! Satan has infused modern religion and the greater body of messiah with a false theology that has divided the body and caused a profound hatred and rejection of the Jewish people and Israel. Satan's plan is an Anti-Semitic teaching called "Church Replacement Theology".

Church Replacement Theology is a prevalent Christian theology. Replacement Theology teaches that Jews killed Christ vice the sin of humanity. Replacement Theology teaches that God is done with Israel and the Church has replaced Israel and the Jewish people[2]. The end result of this false theology is this; Since the Church has replaced Israel there's no need to share the Gospel with Jews because God is done with them!

Most people are aware that this is also a fundamental teaching of Islam. This explains the fundamental Islamic hatred and persecution of Israel and the Jewish people. Replacement Theology also explains the Church's historical Anti-Semitism. The existence of the Jewish people and the nation of Israel are unexplainable and stand as a constant irritant to those who teach Replacement Theology. This is why so many (even some Christians) seek to eliminate Israel and the Jewish People. This commonality alone should be a clarion call, a warning sign of great danger to the greater Church! How can any Church teaching be in agreement with Islam or against the word of God? Scripture warns against this.

> *"Do not yoke yourselves together in a team with unbelievers. For how can righteousness and lawlessness be partners? What fellowship does light have with darkness?"*
> **II Corinthians 6:14**

All "replacement" theology is a lie of Satan. God clearly states that He's not done with Israel. God is a covenant God who never rescinds His own words or promises! So why does replacement theology exist? The answer is simple. If Israel doesn't receive Yeshua, Jesus the Jewish Messiah, they won't call upon Him to return. If Yeshua doesn't return, Satan doesn't go to jail for a thousand years. This is what it's all about! Replacement Theology is Satan's attempt to thwart Yeshua's return because Satan will go to jail for a thousand years!

This is why so many denominations won't witness to Jews despite God's command to share the Gospel "to the Jew First".

Satan's deceptive plan is so crystal clear when plumbed against God's word that it's hard to comprehend why any believer would succumb to the deception of Replacement Theology. Satan's plan also reveals the struggle over the physical land of Israel and the holy city of Jerusalem! When Israel calls out "Blessed is He who comes in the name of the Lord" Yeshua will return to Jerusalem! Dividing the Land of Israel (Land for Peace policies) and dividing Jerusalem to make a Muslim capitol is Satan's secondary, back-up plan[3]. If Satan fails to keep the Church from evangelizing Jewish people, he'll attempt to destroy and divide Yeshua's place of return and throne of authority, Jerusalem! The question looms, whose plan are you and your church following? God's or Satan's!

VIII. God's plan.

Let's bring this all together. The fact that a remnant of the Messianic Jewish community remains today is proof that the bible is absolute truth and at work in our world today. Satan has diligently worked overtime in the last 3,500 years to prevent Israel from fulfilling its prophetic destiny to be a light unto the world, to be God's evangelists and spiritual authority here on earth, to be the land, culture, and people through which God would bring salvation to the world through His Son Yeshua. This is God's protocol. Satan seeks to destroy God's plans concerning His land and people. Satan wants to eliminate the culture and land to whom Yeshua will return. Why? Because when Jesus returns He will judge the nations from the Holy city of Jerusalem. God's plan for believers isn't limited to their salvation alone. God commands every believer to be actively advancing His Kingdom into the world. Believers are not to be sitting on their hands waiting for His Son's return!

> "Since everything is going to be destroyed like this, what kind of people should you be? You should lead holy and godly lives, [12]as you wait for the Day of God and work to hasten its coming. That Day will bring on the destruction of the heavens by fire, and the elements will melt from the heat."
> **II Peter 3:11-12**

The key phrase in this scripture is "work to hasten its coming". Hasten in the Greek is "Speudo", which means that which was meant for later to come now! This is revolutionary and earth shattering! We are to work to hasten Yeshua's return not just sit on the sidelines doing nothing! How can we hasten the return of Messiah? When the worldwide Church fulfills its biblical calling to share the "Good News", the Gospel with the Jewish People (**Romans 1:16**), a worldwide Jewish revival will occur which will then cause Israel to cry out, "Blessed is he who comes in the name of ADONAI" (**Matthew 23:39**).

These are the exact words Yeshua said would cause Him to return to Earth! This seems so simple yet so few, so very few Christians are engaged in fulfilling God's plan. You can hasten Yeshua's return by sharing Yeshua with your Jewish friend, doctor, lawyer, dentist, neighbor, or co-worker. Don't be a spectator; get involved in God's work to hasten Yeshua's return! Share the "Good News" with a Jewish person today!

Chapter Four Notes

1. Kumar, V. M., Mallick, B. N., Chhina, G. S., & Singh, B. (1984). "*Influence of Ascending Reticular Activating System On Preoptic Neuronal-Activity*"

2. R. Kendall Soulen, "*The God of Israel and Christian Theology*", Minneapolis: Fortress, 1996.

3. United Nations Security Council Resolution 242

— Chapter 5 —

America's Prophetic Destiny as a Nation

I. The One New Man.

The Grand Republic of America was founded on Judeo/Christian principles taken directly from the bible. Contrary to revisionist historians (modern day historians who change historical facts for political purposes), America is a nation founded upon biblical principles, morals, and lifestyles as commanded by the God[1]. America has a Godly, divine prophetic purpose.

> *"Note, however, that the body from the Spirit did not come first, but the ordinary human one; the one from the Spirit comes afterwards"* **I Corinthians 15:46**

Sha'ul (Paul) states first the natural then the spiritual. The first permanent settlement in America was the colony of Jamestown established on Jamestown Island on May13th, 1607. The initial name of this colony was Virginia whose territory stretched from the Atlantic seaboard to the Pacific coast; all of North America was initially the colony of Virginia. The colonial capitol was Jamestown until it was moved to Williamsburg, Virginia in 1699. The 400th anniversary of America's birth at Jamestown was celebrated in the spring of 2007. Tav is the Hebrew letter for 400 and stands for truth! There is a strong biblical and spiritual significance of this 400 year cycle.

God promised Abraham that his descendents would acquire the promise land after 400 years (Genesis 15). The year 2007 was America's 400th anniversary. Just like God's promise to Abraham which culminated in Israel's entering into the promise land. The most divine and amazing aspect of the landing at Jamestown in 1607 were the covenant promises of the "One New Man" (Jew and Gentile) that was planted and released in a prayer that was spoken twice a day at the main gate, the Eastern gate of Jamestown Fort.

II. God's Plan Results In The Fulfillment of the Promise.

Right now many of you reading this are asking, "What is the "One New Man"? Ephesians chapter two gives a complete explanation.

"Therefore, remember your former state: you Gentiles by birth—called the Uncircumcised by those who, merely because of an operation on their flesh, are called the Circumcised—[12]at that time had no Messiah. You were estranged from the national life of Isra'el. You were foreigners to the covenants embodying God's promise. You were in this world without hope and without God. [13]But now, you who were once far off have been brought near through the shedding of the Messiah's blood. [14]For he himself is our shalom —he has made us both one and has broken down the m'chitzah which divided us [15]by destroying in his own body the enmity occasioned by the Torah, with its commands set

forth in the form of ordinances. He did this in order to create in union with himself from the two groups a single new humanity and thus make shalom, [16]and in order to reconcile to God both in a single body by being executed on a stake as a criminal and thus in himself killing that enmity. [17]Also, when he came, he announced as Good News shalom to you far off and shalom to those nearby, [18]news that through him we both have access in one Spirit to the Father. [19]So then, you are no longer foreigners and strangers. On the contrary, you are fellow-citizens with God's people and members of God's family." **Ephesians 2:11-19**

This scripture reveals God's plan which was formerly hidden but has now been reveled through His disciples. God was not only reconciling His own people, the Jewish people back unto Himself through Yeshua's death and resurrection, He was also reconciling the Gentiles unto Himself as well! Remember, this is the prophetic calling of the Jewish people, "To be a light unto the nations". Because the Jewish people had a relationship with God and the Gentiles did not, there arose a wall of separation (m'chitzah in Hebrew) between Jews and Gentiles, a wall of animosity (separation).

God sent Jesus to the earth for this unity outlined in Ephesians chapter two. Yeshua taught this unity, and died for this unity. God is reconciling unto Himself both Jewish and Gentile believers through His Son as "One New Man", One New Humanity, and One Bride! We know Biblically that it is God's heart that we (Jew and Gentile) become one through Messiah Yeshua. I would like to show you a prophetic revelation of the "One New Man" found in Numbers Chapter 13 and 14. Twelve spies, one from each tribe, were sent into the Promise Land to reconnoiter the land and the inhabitants.

"Moshe and Aharon fell on their faces before the entire assembled community of the people of Isra'el. ⁶Y'hoshua the son of Nun and Kalev the son of Y'funeh, from the detachment that had reconnoitered the land, tore their clothes ⁷and said to the whole community of Isra'el, The land we passed through in order to spy it out is an outstandingly good land! ⁸If ADONAI is pleased with us, then he will bring us into this land and give it to us—a land flowing with milk and honey. ⁹Just don't rebel against ADONAI. And don't be afraid of the people living in the land—we'll eat them up! Their defense has been taken away from them, and ADONAI is with us! Don't be afraid of them!" ¹⁰But just as the whole community were saying they should be stoned to death, the glory of ADONAI appeared in the tent of meeting to all the people of Isra'el." **Numbers 14:5-10**

This passage records the children of Israel's refusal to enter into and conquer the promise land as God had ordered. The Israelites chose instead to send spies and reconnoiter the land, even though God had already given it to them. God spoke unto Moses and said "Sh'lach l'cha" (Hebrew for send for yourselves) spies. God didn't need spies. He had already made known His promise. This spirit of hardened hearts and rebellion that Israel displayed is still prevalent today among those serving the Lord! Through Yeshua we have God's promise of healing, wholeness, restored relationships, restored marriages, restored minds, broken curses, release from addictions, and every one of our provisions met! The promises are ours, given to us by Yeshua! Many today fail to claim these promises. This is why we are so often not victorious, our hearts are hardened. We hesitate, reconnoiter, and attempt to send spies to scout our problems and situations. We search for a way around them instead of claiming victory over and conquering them as

God has promised us! We don't have to send spies or reconnoiter as Yeshua has already won the battle and given us all authority!

The twelve spies were sent to reconnoiter the promise land for 40 days. Upon their return they brought reports of abundant crops and a cluster of grapes so large that it took two men to carry it on their shoulders slung on a pole. Despite _seeing_ the evidence of "milk and honey" as God had promised, ten of the twelve spies reported to Moses and the people that the land was filled with large giants who made the Israelites look like tiny grasshoppers. They reported that the land "could not be taken". Considering the miracles God had just performed in the Exodus from Egypt, it's nearly impossible to comprehend why the Israelites cried out "it would have been better to stay in Egypt" even though they knew God was with them. God proved His presence was with them through all His miracles! You could take them out of Egypt but you couldn't take Egypt out of them!

Two very famous spies of the twelve, Joshua (also known as Ephraim Hosea, son of Nun) and Kalev (Caleb) make a very different report. Kalev said in Numbers 13:30 "Kalev silenced the people around Moshe and said, "We ought to go up immediately and take possession of it; there is no question that we can conquer it." God's anger flared at those who balked at taking possession of the land and the entire generation over the age of 20 that had been slaves in Egypt would perish in the wilderness and never enter the land. Kalev and Joshua however found favor with the Lord for their faith, belief, and their representation of the Lord. These two men of God were allowed to enter the Promise Land and receive their inheritance!

Now, here's the "One New Man" scriptural revelation! Kalev was not Jewish! He was a Kenizzite (**Numbers 32:12**); a group of people from the area North and East of the land of Israel in what is now present day Syria. Kalev was a proselytite, a convert to Judaism and the Jewish People. Kalev was integrated into the tribe of Judah and was selected as one of the twelve spies. Kalev and Joshua were the first "One New Man" in the bible, a Jew and Gentile who came together as one to inherit God's promises given through Abraham. Not only were Joshua and Kalev the first "One New Man", they were the only two of the twelve spies who said the land could and should be taken. The promises, the fullness, and the completeness of the Kingdom of God are for the Jew and Gentile, bound together as one through the blood of Yeshua! It is the "One New Man" who will enter God's rest in Hebrews 4:6-11. Yeshua's plan for us is to stand together as One! Joshua and Kalev set a heavenly example for us to follow to receive our inheritance from God!

God's plan, God's word, God's Son Yeshua never mentions dual streams of worship consisting of the Church and the Messianic Synagogue. Yeshua didn't die for us to be in two separate but equal camps, that's called Jim Crow or Apartide. Division is of Satan, unity is of God. Yeshua was crucified so that **WE (believing Jew and believing Gentile) WOULD BE ONE!** There is a transition period during which the Church and the Messianic Synagogue will acknowledge each other and recognize their commonalities but that's not the end effect God seeks. The word is specific that Yeshua returns for a bride, a body comprised of Jewish and Gentile believers. The key in understanding the "One New Man" outpouring is that each people groups retains their cultural identity. Those who are Jewish continue being Jews, those who are African American continue being African American, those who are First Nations people continue in their identity as First Nations people, those who are Irish continue to be Irish and so forth! This is a fatal Christian mistake that has caused a majority of missions work in the greater body of Messiah to fail over the centuries. Becoming

"Joint Heirs" of the Kingdom of God through Yeshua does not require you to lose your cultural identity, there's no "Conversion". God embraces and celebrates diversity, **HE CREATED OUR DIVERSITY**. The Church must realize humanities cultural diversity and teach biblical holiness, purity, and righteousness living vice European ethnic and cultural lifestyle. Scripture records One God, One Son, One Holy Spirit, and One Bride not many!

The One New Man is **_not_** the Church in unity with unsaved Israel. This is a critical point that is problematic within the Church today. Yeshua said believing Gentiles are to be in unity with believing Jews, not unbelieving Jews or Orthodox Jews. Paul states in Romans Chapter Eleven that the gentile calling is to "provoke" unsaved Jews to jealousy. That means sharing the "Good News" of Yeshua. Fellowship and relationship is inherently critical to sharing the Gospel but there should never be times or events of ministry or fellowship with unsaved Jewish people in which evangelism, the sharing of Yeshua is restricted, inhibited, or even not allowed.

The gentile calling is not accomplished or fulfilled by the Church giving Orthodox Jews and their Rabbis millions upon millions of U.S. dollars annually at the expense of the Messianic Jew. Orthodox Jews will not participate in any program, event, or service that includes Messianic Jews. The Church today so desperately wants to fellowship with Israel that they will oppress and disregard the Jewish believer for a relationship with an unsaved Jew. This is contrary to scripture which specifically calls for Christians to stand with **Messianic Jews** spiritually, physically, and financially.

> *"They were pleased to do it, but the fact is that they owe it to them. For if the Gentiles have shared with the Jews in spiritual matters, then the Gentiles clearly have a duty to help the Messianic Jews in material matters."* **Romans 15:27**

Yeshua prayed five times in the High Priestly prayer of John 17 for "these" (who are the Jewish talmidim, followers of Yeshua, Messianic Jews) and "those" (Gentiles who would come to faith in Yeshua by "them" Yeshua's Jewish talmidim evangelizing) would be **ONE!** When "these" and "those" become one, Yeshua said something supernatural will happen.

> *"That they may all be one. Just as you, Father, are united with me and I with you, I pray that they may be united with us, so that the world may believe that you sent me"* **John 17:21**

Yeshua said that when Jewish and Gentile believers become one "the world may believe that you sent me". This is a profound revelation of the end days. When we (Believing Jew and Believing Gentile) become one **THE WORLD WILL KNOW**, we will experience a **WORLD WIDE MOVE OF GOD!** Yeshua gave us the formula for **WORLD WIDE REVIVAL!**

III. The Prayer of Jamestown.

Now that you have a clear understanding of what the "One New Man" is, let's read a portion of a prayer that was recited at the Eastern Gate, the Main Gate to Jamestown Fort from approximately 1609 until the year 1699.

The following is a direct quote from that prayer exactly as it was written and published in England titled "Lawes Divine, Morall and Martiall for the Colony of Virginea"-Printed in the year 1612 "A Praier duly said Morning and Evening upon the Court of Guard, either by the Captaine of the watch himselfe, or by some one of his principall officers. (The bold and underlined was added by me to emphasize this point of the prayer).

> *"We beseech thee to furnish the Churches with faithfull and fruitfull ministers, and to blesse their lives and labours*

for those mercifull uses, to which thou hast ordained them, sanctifie thy people O God, and let them not deceive themselves with a formalitie of religion in steed of the power thereof, give them grace to profit both by those favours, and by those chasticements which thou hast sent successively or mixedly amongst them. And Lord represse that rage of sinne, and prophanesse in all Christian states which breeds so much Apostacy and defection, threatning the taking away of this light from them: Confound thou O God all the counsel and practices of Satan and his ministers, which are or shall be taken up against thee, and the kingdome of thy deare sonne. ***And call in the Jewes together with the fulnesse of the gentiles, that thy name may be glorious in al the world, the dayes of iniquity may come to an end, and we with all thine elect people may come to see thy face in glorie, and be filled with the light thereof for evermore.***"

This prayer establishes God's purpose and divine destiny for the Nation of America. This prayer, spoken twice a day for 90 years saturated the soil and airwaves of this nation. This prayer established the spiritual DNA, the genetic foundation and purpose of America. The "One New Man" is the reason God has given America such cultural sway among the nations. God purposed America to model the "One new Man" to the world which will provoke Israel to jealousy and Salvation. America is a cultural melting pot of cultures and people. This melting pot became a believing nation based upon God's word whose diversity would enable true unity between believing Jew and believing Gentile.

"Today I have placed you over nations and kingdoms to uproot and to tear down, to destroy and to demolish, to build and to plant." **Jeremiah 1:10**

God builds up and tears down Nations. God's reason for raising up America to its heights of greatness and global influence was not to create another "superpower". His purpose was to build a Godly Nation established upon His word to be a unified body of Jewish and Gentile believers (inclusive of all cultures from the earth) in Yeshua who will provoke unsaved Jewish people to faith in Yeshua and will stand with Israel. I must place a caveat here that this is not a Unitarian concept which espouses a pluralistic, universalism, the theology of many paths to numerous names to God which includes atheism. The "One New Man" unity is based upon the foundational principles of God's word, ALL of God's word!

When my friend Pastor Wade Trump in Jamestown, Virginia gave me a copy of this Jamestown prayer years ago it took me a while to comprehend it! The absolute truth of God's word, His prophetic destiny for this Republic called "America" has been buried under 400 years of dross, skewed history, political correctness, and deceptive lies. All of this is Satan's futile attempt to thwart and undermine God's plan. The message for America and its prophetic destiny at this hour replicates the resounding statement Mordecai made to Queen Esther over 2,500 years ago.

> "...Don't suppose that merely because you happen to be in the royal palace you will escape any more than the other Jews. ¹⁴For if you fail to speak up now, relief and deliverance will come to the Jews from a different direction; but you and your father's family will perish. Who knows whether you didn't come into your royal position precisely for such a time as this."
> **Esther 4:13-14**

God will fulfill His plan according to His word. He will do it with or without us. The lessen we learned from Great Britain in Chapter One must be remembered. By submitting to God's will and authority as a nation and standing with Israel, America will receive His Blessings. If we are disobedient God will move on and choose another nation to fulfill His will! When the "One New Man" is released from the nation of America and broadcast globally, the world will witness and experience the power of God!

The days of iniquity will come to an end and we will see the fullness of His glory! By rebelling against His will and word we will receive God's Judgment instead of His Glory. Joshua spoke my sentiments millennia ago.

> *"If it seems bad to you to serve ADONAI, then choose today whom you are going to serve! Will it be the gods your ancestors served beyond the River? Or the gods of the Emori, in whose land you are living? As for me and my household, we will serve ADONAI!"* **Joshua 24:15**

The question now is "Who will YOU serve?" Will you be obedient to America's calling and destiny to be the model and example of the "One New Man" to Israel and the world?

Chapter Five Notes

1. *"What if Jesus Had Never Been Born"* by Dr. D. James Kennedy and Jerry Newcombe:

Chapter 6

The Olive Tree

I. How is the One New Man Formed?

The "days of iniquity coming to an end" isn't the final purpose of the "One New Man" God is releasing in this hour, it's just the beginning! I mentioned in the Preface that there are some very somber and sobering statistics that reveal the Body of Messiah is in a steep decline across America and the world. We're losing our youth, we are not winning lost souls, and we have lost the ability to influence society. We're dying! How do we breathe life into dead bones? How do we revive a dead and dying Church Body? Paul gives an incredible analogy of the Kingdom of God regarding Jewish and Gentile believers being grafted into the olive tree which represents the greater "House of Israel". Unfortunately, extremely few Pastors teach from this chapter yet it's a foundational keystone that defines the greater body of Messiah.

> *"In that case, I say, isn't it that they have stumbled with the result that they have permanently fallen away? Heaven forbid! Quite the contrary, it is by means of their stumbling that the deliverance has come to the Gentiles, in order to*

provoke them to jealousy. ¹²Moreover, if their stumbling is bringing riches to the world—that is, if Isra'el's being placed temporarily in a condition less favored than that of the Gentiles is bringing riches to the latter—how much greater riches will Isra'el in its fullness bring them! ¹³However, to those of you who are Gentiles I say this: since I myself am an emissary sent to the Gentiles, I make known the importance of my work ¹⁴in the hope that somehow I may provoke some of my own people to jealousy and save some of them! ¹⁵For if their casting Yeshua aside means reconciliation for the world, what will their accepting him mean? It will be life from the dead! ¹⁶Now if the hallah offered as firstfruits is holy, so is the whole loaf. And if the root is holy, so are the branches. ¹⁷But if some of the branches were broken off, and you—a wild olive—were grafted in among them and have become equal sharers in the rich root of the olive tree, ¹⁸then don't boast as if you were better than the branches! However, if you do boast, remember that you are not supporting the root, the root is supporting you. ¹⁹So you will say, "Branches were broken off so that I might be grafted in." ²⁰True, but so what? They were broken off because of their lack of trust. However, you keep your place only because of your trust. So don't be arrogant; on the contrary, be terrified! ²¹For if God did not spare the natural branches, he certainly won't spare you! ²²So take a good look at God's kindness and his severity: on the one hand, severity toward those who fell off; but, on the other hand, God's kindness toward you—provided you maintain yourself in that kindness! Otherwise, you too will be cut off! ²³Moreover, the others, if they do not persist in their lack of trust, will be grafted in; because God is able to graft them back in. ²⁴For if you were cut out of what is by nature a wild olive tree and grafted, contrary to nature, into a cultivated olive tree, how much more will these natural branches be grafted back into their own olive tree! ²⁵For, brothers, I want you to understand this truth which God formerly concealed but has now revealed, so that you won't imagine you know more than you actually do. It is that stoniness, to a degree, has come upon Isra'el, until the Gentile world enters in its fullness; ²⁶and that it is in this way that all Isra'el will be saved. As the Tanakh says, "Out of Tziyon will come the Redeemer; he will turn away ungodliness from Ya'akov ²⁷and this will be my covenant with them, when I take away their sins." ²⁸With respect to the Good News they are hated for your sake. But with respect to being chosen they are loved for the Patriarchs' sake, ²⁹for God's free gifts and his calling are irrevocable. ³⁰Just as you yourselves were disobedient to God before but have received mercy now because of Isra'el's disobedience; ³¹so also Isra'el has been disobedient now, so that by your showing them the same mercy that God has shown you, they too may now receive God's mercy." **Romans 11:11-31**

II. Romans Chapter Eleven breakdown.

Sha'ul's allegory is that the Kingdom of God is comprised of natural and wild Olive branches being either cut off or grafted in to a cultivated Olive Tree which represents Israel. Two Thousand years ago the known world was agrarian. The world's population with a few exceptions lived by farming and hunting, they lived off of the land. Today's populations, with a few exceptions are mostly urban or suburban. This modern lifestyle makes Paul's analogy difficult to understand to those who have little knowledge of farming practices. In Paul's own words this olive tree allegory is a "truth which God formerly concealed but has now revealed". To understand what God is doing in our day regarding the land of Israel and Jewish and Gentile believers we must understand and comprehend Romans Chapter Eleven.

First, Sha'ul states a biblical fact that Israel and the Jewish People have not permanently fallen away From God. Israel's falling away resulted in salvation to the Gentiles. Romans 11:11 also contains the prophetic calling upon the Gentile believer, to provoke Jewish people to jealousy regarding Yeshua. Israel has been provoked these past 1,700 years but not to jealousy of Yeshua!

Paul then goes on to explain that salvation through Yeshua is like being grafted into a Jewish rooted Olive Tree. The Jewish people are referred to as the native branch and Gentiles are referred to as wild olive branches. Olive farming is a staple in Israel and most of the Middle East. A farmer who desires to increase his olive grove (fruit) does so through grafting. Cultivated Olive trees produce fruit (olives) whereas wild olive trees produce small inedible fruit or none at all. To increase his olive grove and production a farmer will graft his olive trees[1]. He will prune (cut off) some native branches of the cultivated olive tree. He takes those cut off branches and places them at the base of the olive tree stump where they lay dormant

> *"In that case, I say, isn't it that they have stumbled with the result that they have permanently fallen away? Heaven forbid!"* **Romans 11:11**

The farmer will find a wild olive tree that has sprouted in the countryside. He will prune or cut off several branches from that wild olive tree and take them back to his cultivated olive grove. With great precision he will drill holes into the cultivated olive tree that he previously pruned. The holes are the exact same diameter as the wild olive branches he just harvested. If the drilled hole is too big the graft won't take, if the hole is too small the branch will not fit into hole drilled into the tree. Trees, like all living organisms God created contain DNA. DNA is an acronym for Deoxyribonucleic acid, the genetic instructions of God in all living organisms. The DNA of the wild olive branch differs from the DNA of the cultivated tree. Because the DNA of the wild branch (which represents the Gentiles) doesn't match the DNA cultivated tree, the branch is unable to draw nourishment from the olive tree root (which represents Israel). The root has to force feed the branch. The wild branch is unable to feed the root through photosynthesis because the DNA doesn't match.

> *"Then don't boast as if you were better than the branches! However, if you do boast, remember that you are not supporting the root, the root is supporting you. ¹⁹So you will say, "Branches were broken off so that I might be grafted in." ²⁰True, but so what? They were broken off because of their lack of trust. However, you keep your place only because of your trust. So don't be arrogant; on the contrary, be terrified!"*
> **Romans 11:18-20**

The cultivated olive tree with the grafted in wild branch is left alone for a period in order for the grafting to take and heal. The root is force-feeding the branch during this time without receiving nourishment. A similar situation occurs in human organ transplant recipients. The blood type must match but the DNA doesn't. The recipient body will always battle to reject the foreign organ because the DNA doesn't match. A transplant patient must take drugs the rest of their life to combat the bodies attempt to reject the transplanted organ with the foreign DNA.

When the wild graft has healed, the farmer grafts the native branch which had been lying dormant at the base of the tree. Because the natural branch is grafted back into its own trunk and the DNA matches, the natural branch immediately begins receiving rich nourishment from the root. The natural branch, revived from dormancy, begins photosynthesizing and immediately begins feeding the root which because the natural branch and the root DNA matches.[2] If the native branch is not grafted back into its native root the olive tree will die, unable to feed its self with only the wild olive branch.

> *"For if their casting Yeshua aside means reconciliation for the world, what will their accepting him mean? It will be life from the dead!"* **Romans 11:15**

There is another process that occurs when both the wild and cultivated branch have been grafted into the cultivated olive tree. The natural branch, sensing the DNA of the grafted wild branch is provoked to jealousy. This is the actual terminology used by horticulturists in describing the olive tree grafting process. This provocation causes an explosive increase in tree growth and nutrient production resulting in a thousand-fold harvest of fruit at the end of the completed grafting process of both the natural and the wild branch.[3]

> *"For if you were cut out of what is by nature a wild olive tree and grafted, contrary to nature, into a cultivated olive tree, how much more will these natural branches be grafted back into their own olive tree!"* **Romans 11:24**

Sha'ul's olive tree analogy is profound and nothing short of supernatural revelation. The mystery that was "once hidden" has now been "revealed". God's plan for world revival is crystal clear. The righteous remnant of Jew and Gentile, the natural and the wild branches grafted into the olive tree together will cause world revival, life from the dead! In Yeshua's own words:

"That they may all be one. Just as you, Father, are united with me and I with you, I pray that they may be united with us, so that the world may believe that you sent me." **John 17:21**

The properly grafted Olive Tree produces a worldwide harvest of fruit. However, there is a grave warning communicated in Paul's teaching to the greater body today coupled with great urgency. Time is running short; the grafted branch cannot feed the root indefinitely. The olive tree is dying without the natural branch to sustain it. This is the very reason the Church is dying today. Unable to feed the root the nourishing power is draining from the root. It is imperative that the natural branch be grafted back into the tree, this is the very reason Yeshua was crucified.

"And in order to reconcile to God both in a single body by being executed on a stake as a criminal and thus in himself killing that enmity." **Ephesians 2:16**

It's time to end replacement theology, Anti-Semitism, and division within the greater body and reach out to the native branch to save the tree! Jewish revival equals world revival! The restoration of the native branch (Israel) back into the olive tree is God's plan of breathing life into the dead, for a worldwide harvest! America's destiny is the release of the One New Man and this is how the One New Man is birthed! Yet today the greater body of Messiah is not experiencing life from the dead. Understanding the Jewish roots of Christianity is not enough; it's not the end goal. God's desire is the grafting process which brings life to the dead and is America's prophetic calling. Why are we not experiencing this, why are we not living it, and will we? It's God's plan, the question looms, is it your plan? Is it your churches plan?

III. Fulfilling Gods plan.

Many faithful and steadfast believers around the world are whole-heartedly seeking God. They are aware of His plans and the prophetic significance of physical Israel in these end days. To experience the presence of God and begin worldwide revival there are three metrics from the book of Joshua regarding Gods vision and mission for this hour that we must abide by before God can restore all things.

> "After the death of Moshe the servant of ADONAI, ADONAI said to Y'hoshua the son of Nun, Moshe's assistant, ²Moshe my servant is dead. So now, get up and cross over this Yarden, you and all the people, to the land I am giving to them, the people of Isra'el. ³I am giving you every place you will step on with the sole of your foot, as I said to Moshe. ⁴All the land from the desert and the L'vanon to the great river, the Euphrates River—all the land of the Hitti—and on to the Great Sea in the west will be your territory. ⁵No one will be able to withstand you as long as you live. Just as I was with Moshe, so I will be with you. I will neither fail you nor abandon you." **Joshua 1:1-5**

1. We must listen for and hear the Lord's voice. Joshua's role as Commander in Chief of Israel necessitated his hearing the Lord's voice. God is calling for unity in this hour between Messianic Jews and believing Gentiles (Christians). Is the body of Messiah listening?

2. There must be obedience to God's vision and mission. Hearing the voice of God is just the beginning, obedience to it is critical. As Sha'ul stated it's not the hearer of the word but the doer. Head knowledge of the One New Man is not

enough; we must begin walking it out, living it according to God's word!

3. Accountability must be restored to the body of Messiah, the Church. God provided a plan and anointing for Joshua to lead Israel into the promise land. If an attempt is made to alter the plans of God (often attempted by man), it thwarts the ministry God called forth. God births and raises up many different ministries and callings for specific times and periods but the "One New Man" is a heavenly birthed move of God that will effect worldwide revival. The anointing to fulfill God's plan cannot be used for a man made plan.

YOU CANNOT UTILIZE GOD'S ANOINTING FOR AN OUTPOURING OF HEAVEN FOR A MAN MADE PLAN FOR HIS OWN PURPOSE!

This error occurs all too often in ministry! A Pastor, a Congregation or church, or even a person or people will cry out to God for His presence and glory. When God hears and answers their prayers and intercessions they often don't like the response, the flavor, or the look of God's plan so they attempt to use the Anointing God gives to carry out their own man-made plan that fits into their own earthly, fleshly desire and understanding. This then causes God's plan to fail. Then, when it does fail the Clergy, Congregation or person will blame God when in reality it's their own fault. God has released the anointing to fulfill His will regarding America's destiny as a nation which is to be the world's example and model of the One New Man, the reconciliation of the Messianic Jew and the believing Gentile into one body, one bride! So often we make it about the bride and not the bridegroom! Don't misuse Gods' anointing for man's desire or plan!

Chapter Six Notes

1. Ferguson, Louise, G. Steven Sibbett and George C. Martin. "*Olive Production Manual*". University of California, Division of Agriculture and Natural Resources: Publication 3353. 1994

2. Hartmann, H.T., K. W. Opitz and J. A. Beutel. "*Olive Production in California*." University of California, Agricultural Sciences Publications: Leaflet 2474. 1980.

3. Klein, Maggie Blyth. "*The Feast of the Olive*". Chronicle Books. 1994

— Chapter 7 —

The Restoration of All Things!

I. What now?

In Acts Chapter three, Kefa (Peter) is addressing a group of Jewish worshippers at the Temple in a portico called Solomon's Colonnade. This group of Jewish worshippers is in complete amazement by a man with whom they were all familiar with, who was born lame and habitually begged at Gate Beautiful for a living. This day however, something was going to be different. Scripture records the story.

> *"A man crippled since birth was being carried in. Every day people used to put him at the Beautiful Gate of the Temple, so that he could beg from those going into the Temple court"* **Acts 3:2**

Life drastically changed for the crippled man the day he met Kefa (Peter)! Peter gave the crippled man **Heaven!**

This supernatural healing occurs just a short period after Yeshua's crucifixion, resurrection, and the great outpouring of the Ruach HaKodesh (Holy Spirit) on Pentecost (Shavuot) in the upper room. Still, the people didn't get it; they didn't understand that the Kingdom of God had come! Kefa responds to the people's amazement that this cripple has just been healed. His response gives us a key revelation of what is occurring in our day regarding the release of the One New Man and accompanying signs and wonders..

> *"Therefore, repent and turn to God, so that your sins may be erased;* [20]*so that times of refreshing may come from the Lord's presence; and he may send the Messiah appointed in advance for you, that is, Yeshua.* [21]*He has to remain in heaven until the time comes for restoring everything, as God said long ago, when he spoke through the holy prophets."* **Acts 3:18-21**

II. A Restoration to what?

Clearly God desires that you and I have periods of refreshing and revival. The purpose of revival is to prepare the bride for return of the groom, Yeshua, to establish the millennial reign. The key mentioned is the hindrance in verse 21. Yeshua has to remain in heaven until the time for restoring everything occurs! What does this mean and what is the impact on the greater body of Messiah? To answer these questions we must first review how the body has gotten to where it is today and why restoration is necessary!

From the time Yeshua was born until the "Council of Nycea"[1] in 325 A.D. the body of Messiah maintained a biblical culture (it was Jewish). The body of Messiah for the first three hundred years past Yeshua's crucifixion kept Shabbat, celebrated the feast days and maintained Jerusalem as the center of their worship and culture (even after the temple was destroyed).

The First Council of Nicea was convened in 325 CE (AD) by Constantine, Emperor of the Roman Empire. Constantine, a worshipper of the Roman "Sun God," purportedly "converted" to Christianity. His reign as Caesar marked a merge of Roman pagan religious customs with the church. Followers of the Way (Messianic Jews and Gentile Believers) were no longer persecuted by the Roman Empire. Instead, the body of Messiah became fractionalized with the various factions persecuting each other with a zeal and vengeance that would shock non-believers!

Constantine, twelve months after his convening the Council of Nicea and his purported conversion to Christianity had his own son Crispus murdered then suffocated his wife Fausta to death.

By the time the council of Nicea was convened in 325 CE, anti-Semitism was already rapidly expanding throughout the Roman Empire and among the Gentiles of the movement[2]. The Council of Nicea, attended by 318 non-Jewish bishops excluded Jews, even forbidding Jews from attending the council. Jews weren't welcome despite the fact the Jerusalem was still considered the center of faith and the Messianic Jewish expression of faith was done in all the Congregations across the Empire of Rome.

The wealthier Roman and Greek congregations were mixing pagan Greco/Roman beliefs, Greek Philosophy and Bible teachings with Constantine's blessing. Constantine needed to consolidate his divided kingdom and throne among the Messianic Congregations and the cultic pagan worship throughout the empire. These cultic worshippers wanted to celebrate their own Greek culture holidays altering the focal point of worship from Jerusalem to Constantinople and eventually Rome when Constantinople fell to the Muslims under Sultan Mehmed II in 1453 C.E[3].

The bishops that attended the Council of Nicea were political appointees of Constantine from the Babylonian Kirk that worshiped Nimrod. This council was unanimous in their decision to move the celebration of Passover to the first Sunday after Passover, which always falls on the 14th of Aviv (Nisan). The mere mention of Passover (Pesach) became distasteful to the Gentile church, and the term "Easter" (from the Greco/Roman goddess of fertility Ishtar) was adopted in place of Passover.

Prior to Constantine, Julius Caesar was officially recognized as the head of the Romanized form of this religion. Julius Caesar was given the title of Pontifex Maximus[4] which means "supreme bridge or being" between man and gods. Each consecutive Roman Caesar held this title including Constantine. Emperor Gratian, Constantine's successor, refused the title when crowned in 376 CE. Instead, he transferred the title to the Bishop of Rome. The Bishop of Rome evolved into the Catholic Pope and retains the title of Pontifex Maximus to this day. Constantine ordered that this new composite religion be the only official and lawful religion throughout the Roman Empire. This is not the first time this type of assimilation has happened in biblical history. Northern Israel was conquered by Ashur (Assyria) in 722 B.C. Most of the Israelites were taken into exile in Ashur (Assyria) while the King attempted to repopulate the Shomron region with citizens from Ashur. They prostituted the word of God with their own pagan customs as well.

"So they feared ADONAI, while at the same time they appointed for themselves priests from among themselves to preside at the high places, and they would sacrifice for them in the temples on the high places. [33] They both feared ADONAI and served their own gods in the manner customary among the nations from which they had been taken away. [34] To this day they continue to follow their former [pagan] customs. They

do not fear ADONAI. They do not follow the regulations, rulings, Torah or mitzvah which ADONAI ordered the descendants of Ya'akov, to whom he gave the name Isra'el."
II Kings 17:32-34

HaSatan's deception has prostituted over two thousand years of God's word, history, culture, and life. This unholy merger of Constantine caused the Holy Spirit to depart from the greater body effectively rendering it powerless. The miraculous, supernatural Messianic Jewish body comprised of believing Jews and believing Gentiles that worshipped the God of Israel according to His word and culture. The same body that had experienced untold signs and wonders as recorded in Acts Chapter 2-6 died, killed through Hellenism as ordered by Constantine's Council of Nicea in 325 A.D.

The Council of Nicea was the Antithesis of the Council of Jerusalem in A.D. 50 where the Gentiles were welcomed into the body with open arms by James the Just-Yeshua's brother as recorded in Acts.

"Therefore, my opinion is that we should not put obstacles in the way of the Goyim who are turning to God."
Acts 15:21

God has given a strong prophetic word concerning the infusion of Hellenism (Greco/Roman philosophy) into the Body of Messiah.

"For I have bent Y'hudah as my bow and made Efrayim its arrow. I will rouse your sons, Tziyon, and make you like a warrior's sword against your sons, Greece." **Zechariah 9:13**

God is raising up the sons of Zion to defeat the sons of Greece. We are still fighting this battle today against Hellenism.

This struggle is the story of Hanukah in which the Syrian Greeks tried to destroy the biblical based culture of Israel by outlawing the word of God and making it a crime to live a biblical lifestyle. Hellenism was the root source of the Council of Nicea.

The Council of Nicea's rulings resulted in the loss of the "Supernatural" within the greater body. The Messianic Congregation morphed into the Church from the Council of Nicea edicts. The newly formed church endeavored to quickly rid itself of biblical culture, customs, and Jewish believers. This resulted in the Church becoming an emaciated, religious facade of the previous "Glorious Body of Messiah" Yeshua had left a little over 300 years earlier. This Hellenism based morphing of the body of Messiah coupled with the fall of the Roman Empire caused the world to plunge into a period that history records as the "Dark Ages"[5]. A time of great spiritual darkness that would last until the early 1600's.

My reasoning for including this brief historical dissertation is not to insult or offend the greater Church, it's Clergy, or Christians. This information is included because we must sift through history to discover how and why the Church's power is dying today. We now understand why Acts 3:21 states that Yeshua's return is hindered until the "time of restoration". The Church's ever increasing interest in the "Jewish Roots" of the Faith is evidence of God's hand in restoring Biblical truth and removing Hellenism from His body! Yeshua Himself confronted similar man-made Hellenistic teachings 2,000 years ago.

> *"He answered, Indeed, why do you break the command of God by your tradition? [4]For God said, `Honor your father and mother,' and `Anyone who curses his father or mother must be put to death.' [5]But you say, `If anyone says to his father or mother, I have promised to give to God what I might*

have used to help you, ⁶then he is rid of his duty to honor his father or mother'. Thus by your tradition you make null and void the word of God!" **Matthew15:3-6**

The greater body must confront its Hellenistic traditions that are not from God or His word. False religion and Hellenistic based teachings oppress and strangle the greater body, resulting in apostasy from God and His word. For the most part the Hellenistic culture, traditions, and teachings remain unchallenged within the Church today. They are like a "pink elephant" sitting in the middle of a crowded living room. Everyone sees it, everyone acknowledges it's presence (a few even know how it got there) but no one dares to talk about it and many don't want it removed! No one has the chutzpah (Yiddish word for audacity) to confront the issues and challenge the "Status Quo" so nothing changes. Decade after decade passes and the spiritual health of the church continues to decline. Let's get this Hellenism out into the open and shed the light of Yeshua upon it and the truth of what the word ***REALLY*** says! Lets hunger for that truth and righteousness vice Hellenism and denial. Let's acknowledge the issue so we may begin the difficult and sensitive task of healing and restoration. We need immediate corrective action to repair the errors and shortcomings of Hellenism within the greater body of Messiah.

"He who spurns discipline detests himself, but he who listens to correction grows in understanding." **Proverbs 15:32**

The body of Messiah must remain teachable, open, and humble in order to receive true biblical restoration. Scripture reveals that in the world to come (the acharit-hayamim in Hebrew) we are to stay away from people like this.

"Moreover, understand this: in the acharit-hayamim will come trying times. ²People will be self-loving, money-loving, proud, arrogant, insulting, disobedient to parents, ungrateful, unholy, ³heartless, unappeasable, slanderous, uncontrolled, brutal, hateful of good, ⁴traitorous, headstrong, swollen with conceit, loving pleasure rather than God, ⁵as they retain the outer form of religion but deny its power. Stay away from these people!" **II Timothy 3:1-5**

Albert Einstein said, "doing the same thing over and over again and expecting different results is the definition of insanity". Hellenistic based theology and programs have been strangling the church for the past 1,700 years resulting in the greater body of Messiah losing their "First Love".

III. Our First Love is Veiled!

"To the angel of the Messianic Community in Ephesus, write: 'Here is the message from the one who holds the seven stars in his right hand and walks among the seven gold menorahs: ²I know what you have been doing, how hard you have worked, how you have persevered, and how you can't stand wicked people; so you tested those who call themselves emissaries but aren't—and you found them to be liars. ³You are persevering, and you have suffered for my sake without growing weary. ⁴But I have this against you: you have lost the love you had at first. ⁵Therefore, remember where you were before you fell, turn from this sin, and do what you used to do before. Otherwise, I will come to you and remove your menorah from its place—if you don't turn from your sin!" **Revelation 2:1-5**

Yeshua states to the Messianic Community in Ephesus that He has this against them; they have "lost their first love" and it's a sin! Yeshua doesn't say what that first love is! To discover what the "First Love" is we must know the background of Ephesus and the Messianic congregation Sha'ul seeded there.

Caesar Augustus became emperor of Rome in 27 B.C. He made Ephesus the provincial capital of this area of the Roman Empire. Ephesus was the provincial seat of the governor and grew into a major metropolis and center of commerce. Ephesus quickly grew to be second only in size and status to Rome itself. It's estimated that Ephesus's population in the year A.D. 100 was 400,000 to 500,000 people. Ephesus reached its commercial and geopolitical zenith during this time period.[6]

Sha'ul lived in Ephesus from 52-54 A.D. Sha'ul wrote a letter to Ephesus while he was imprisoned in Rome around A.D. 62. This letter became known as the New Testament (B'rit Hadasha) Book of Ephesians. Sha'ul's journey to Ephesus is recorded in Acts 19:

> *"While Apollos was in Corinth, Sha'ul completed his travels through the inland country and arrived at Ephesus, where he found a few talmidim. [2]He asked them, 'Did you receive the Ruach HaKodesh when you came to trust?' 'No,' they said to him, 'we have never even heard that there is such a thing as the Ruach HaKodesh.' [3]'In that case,' he said, 'into what were you immersed?' 'The immersion of Yochanan,' they answered. [4]Sha'ul said, 'Yochanan practiced an immersion in connection with turning from sin to God; but he told the people to put their trust in the one who would come after him, that is, in Yeshua.' [5]On hearing this, they were immersed into the name of the Lord Yeshua; [6]and when Sha'ul placed his hands on them, the Ruach HaKodesh came upon them; so that they began speaking in tongues and prophesying. [7]In all, there were about twelve of these men. [8]Sha'ul went into the synagogue; and for three months he spoke out boldly, engaging*

in dialogue and trying to persuade people about the Kingdom of God. ⁹But some began hardening themselves and refusing to listen; and when these started defaming the Way before the whole synagogue, Sha'ul withdrew, took the talmidim with him, and commenced holding daily dialogues in Tyrannus's yeshivah. ¹⁰This went on for two years; so that everyone, both Jews and Greeks, living in the province of Asia heard the message about the Lord. **Acts 19:1-10**

Sha'ul reveals what the "First Love" Yeshua mentions in Rev. 2:4 is in his letter to the Ephesians. The overall theme of the Book of Ephesians is the unity and reconciliation of Jew, Gentile, and all creation unto God through His Son Yeshua.

"Therefore, remember your former state: you Gentiles by birth—called the Uncircumcised by those who, merely because of an operation on their flesh, are called the Circumcised—¹²at that time had no Messiah. You were estranged from the national life of Isra'el. You were foreigners to the covenants embodying God's promise. You were in this world without hope and without God. ¹³But now, you who were once far off have been brought near through the shedding of the Messiah's blood. ¹⁴For he himself is our shalom—he has made us both one and has broken down the m'chitzah which divided us ¹⁵by destroying in his own body the enmity occasioned by the Torah, with its commands set forth in the form of ordinances. He did this in order to create in union with himself from the two groups a single new humanity and thus make shalom, ¹⁶and in order to reconcile to God both in a single body by being executed on a stake as a criminal and thus in himself killing that enmity. ¹⁷Also, when he came, he announced as Good News shalom to you far off and shalom to those nearby, ¹⁸news that through him we both have access in one Spirit

to the Father. ¹⁹So then, you are no longer foreigners and
strangers. On the contrary, you are fellow-citizens with God's
people and members of God's family" **Ephesians 2:11-19**

Gentiles had no relationship with God as the Jewish people
did so there arose a conflict between the two, an enmity between
the only two people groups God recognizes, Jew and Gentile. The
Gentiles were estranged from the culture, life, and context of the
national life of Israel. Sha'ul describes this life through the Olive
Tree teaching in Romans chapter 11 (refer to Chapter Six.)

Yeshua's crucifixion reconciled the two people groups together,
which Sha'ul calls the "One New Man" (Eph. 2:15). Gentiles
became joint heirs, adopted children of God in love through
Yeshua's crucifixion. Sha'ul talks about this love in Ephesians
chapter 3.

"And if you read what I have written, you will grasp
how I understand this secret plan concerning the Messiah. ⁵In
past generations it was not made known to mankind, as the
Spirit is now revealing it to his emissaries and prophets, ⁶that
in union with the Messiah and through the Good News the
Gentiles were to be joint heirs, a joint body and joint sharers
with the Jews in what God has promised." **Ephesians 3:4-6**

This revelation of this former secret continues on to Ephesians
chapter four where Sha'ul defines how to become one while
preserving the unity Yeshua died for!

"Always be humble, gentle and patient, bearing with one
another in love, ³and making every effort to preserve the unity
the Spirit gives through the binding power of shalom. ⁴There
is one body and one Spirit, just as when you were called you
were called to one hope. ⁵And there is one Lord, one trust, one

immersion, ⁶*and one God, the Father of all, who rules over all, works through all and is in all."* **Ephesians 4:2-6**

Paul tells us that if we're listening we must strip off the old independent natured self and put on the "One New Man"!

"If you really listened to him and were instructed about him, then you learned that since what is in Yeshua is truth, ²²*then, so far as your former way of life is concerned, you must strip off your old nature, because your old nature is thoroughly rotted by its deceptive desires;* ²³*and you must let your spirits and minds keep being renewed,* ²⁴*and clothe yourselves with the new nature created to be godly, which expresses itself in the righteousness and holiness that flow from the truth."* **Ephesians 4:21-24**

The "One New Man" attire is to be coupled with the infilling of Ruach HaKodesh (Holy Spirit)!

*"Don't get drunk with wine, because it makes you lose control. Instead, keep on being filled with the Spirit—*¹⁹*sing psalms, hymns and spiritual songs to each other; sing to the Lord and make music in your heart to him;* ²⁰*always give thanks for everything to God the Father in the name of our Lord Yeshua the Messiah.* ²¹*Submit to one another in fear of the Messiah."* **Ephesians 5:18-21**

The result is that the "One New Man" unity between Jew and Gentile releases the supernatural power and anointing of God, empowering believers to be Godly warriors, prepared for spiritual battle, and moving in signs and wonders!

"Finally, grow powerful in union with the Lord, in union with his mighty strength! ¹¹*Use all the armor and weaponry that God provides, so that you will be able to stand against the*

deceptive tactics of the Adversary. ¹²For we are not struggling against human beings, but against the rulers, authorities and cosmic powers governing this darkness, against the spiritual forces of evil in the heavenly realm. ¹³So take up every piece of war equipment God provides; so that when the evil day comes, you will be able to resist; and when the battle is won, you will still be standing." **Ephesians 6:10-13**

Finally, to answer the question from Revelation 2:4; What is the "First Love" of Ephesus? It's the same "First Love" as the Messianic Movement of today and of 2,000 years ago, Yeshua the Jewish Messiah! Yeshua died for the salvation of both Jews and Gentiles to unify them into the "One New Man"! That's the first love and it is the first love of the Ephesus congregation as written in Sha'ul's letter to them from Rome in A.D. 62! We must not lose our "First Love" and have our menorah, our light, removed. The ultimate purpose of the this unity is Jewish revival whose ultimate, end result is World revival. Remember the words of Yeshua in

"I united with them and you with me, so that they may be completely one, and the world thus realize that you sent me, and that you have loved them just as you have loved me" **John 17:23**

The world will realize who Yeshua is as Humanities Messiah! A global harvest ensues. Yeshua established the pattern and commands us to go the nations while going first to the Jewish people:

"But go rather to the lost sheep of the house of Isra'el." **Matthew 10:6**

"Therefore, go and make people from all nations into talmidim, immersing them into the reality of the Father, the Son and the Ruach HaKodesh." **Matthew 28:19**

Sha'ul confirms Yeshua's plan and gives the same pattern in Romans Chapter One.

> *"For I am not ashamed of the gospel, for it is the power of God for salvation to everyone who believes, to the Jew first and also to the Greek."* **Romans 1:16**

As I mentioned previously in Chapter Four believers get bogged down with the bureaucracy of their congregation like building programs, children's programs, discipleship programs, training programs, and various teaching and empowering programs which are all necessary for the day to day running of any congregation but it can't overshadow our purpose and destiny! We can't lose our "First Love", our Jewish Messiah who came to bring salvation to the Jewish people and commanded us to do the same!

I am often asked by other Messianic Jews; "Why aren't there more Jews who receive Yeshua?" This is a valid question and one that I will answer in two parts.

1. Most Jewish people don't recognize Yeshua.

> *"The sons of Isra'el came to buy along with the others that came, since the famine extended to the land of Kena'an.* ⁶*Yosef was governor over the land; it was he who sold to all the people of the land. Now when Yosef's brothers came and prostrated themselves before him on the ground,* ⁷*Yosef saw his brothers and recognized them; but he acted toward them as if he were a stranger and spoke harshly with them. He asked them, 'Where are you from?' They answered, 'From the land of Kena'an to buy food.'* ⁸*So Yosef recognized his brothers, but they didn't recognize him."* **Genesis 42:5-8.**

Joseph is a redeemer, a foreshadow of Yeshua. The Babylonian Talmud teaches that two Messiahs would come, one named after

Him; Ben Joseph, the suffering Messiah! [6] The second Messiah to come is named Ben David who will rule the world from Jerusalem. This is a detailed description of Yeshua, who came the first time to suffer and die for our sins. When Yeshua returns His second time here) he will rule in Jerusalem like King David did!

Joseph the dream interpreter, son of Jacob would suffer as well at the hands of his own jealous brothers who sold him into slavery.

Joseph's misfortune eventually results in his becoming the second most powerful man in all of Egypt after Pharaoh. God gave Joseph this powerful position to allow him to bring salvation to his family during a time of great famine. Joseph's position would allow him to provide food to his starving family in the midst of famine as well as the nations of the earth who came to Egypt for the grain that had been stored.

The final key to the first part of the answer lies in verse 8 of Genesis 42, "they didn't recognize him". Joseph's brothers didn't recognize him! Why, because Joseph the Jewish shepherd who was sold into slavery now stood before his brothers dressed as an official of the Egyptian court? Joseph's head is shaved, as was the Egyptian custom. He's wearing Egyptian clothing, probably a wig, and most likely he's wearing eye makeup which members of Pharaohs court usually did! Joseph's brothers didn't recognize him as presented. Joseph was dressed in Egyptian clothing which veiled or cloaked his true Jewish identity from his brothers. They didn't recognize Joseph!

In the last 1,750 years the Church has veiled Yeshua the Jewish Messiah like Egypt did Joseph. The Jewish Yeshua has been transformed into "Jesus Christ" of the Rome based Church. Like Joseph wearing Egyptian clothing, Yeshua, the Jew has been veiled by Hellenistic clothing and teaching to become the Roman's Jesus.

Like Joseph and his brothers, most Jewish people today don't recognize Yeshua because He's dressed like a Roman vice his true Jewish identity.

As Messianic Believers it's our reasonability and calling to remove the veil, the cloak that's disguising and hiding Yeshua Ha Mashiach, the Jewish Messiah! It's one of the main reasons for the reemergence and rebirth of the Messianic Community! The Church's calling according to Romans 11 is to provoke Israel to jealousy. They have been unable to fulfill this calling because they have veiled and hidden Yeshua's true identity. The Church presents a Roman Jesus to Jewish people looking for the Jewish Messiah so they don't recognize or accept Him! Yeshua's true identity as the Jewish Messiah must be revealed to both the church and the Jewish people!

2. Part two of the answer: "Why aren't there more Jews who receive Yeshua?"

Because the Messianic Community isn't fully operating in signs and wonders. Scripture shares what's necessary to reveal the Jewish Messiah to Jewish People: Miracles, Signs and Wonders through the infilling of the Ruach HaKodesh (Holy Spirit)!

> *"Precisely because Jews ask for signs and Greeks try to find wisdom"* **I Corinthians 1:22**

The first outpouring which occurred 2,000 years ago on Shavuot in Jerusalem is recorded in Acts chapter two and reveals the greatest Jewish revival ever known:

> *"So those who accepted what he said were immersed, and there were added to the group that day about three thousand people."* **Acts 2:41**

What sparked this massive revival of Jewish repentance and acceptance of Yeshua? Was it programs? Was it a crusade? Was it door-to-door evangelism? Was it ministry flyers? Was it a weekend seminar? Was it a scheduled church revival? The unequivocal answer to all of these questions is a loud and emphatic **NO!** The actual answer is revealed in verse 4 of Acts Chapter 2.

> *"They were all filled with the Ruach HaKodesh and began to talk in different languages, as the Spirit enabled them to speak"* **Acts 2:4**

The spark of that revival was the Ruach HaKodesh (Holy Spirit)! The infilling of the Ruach occurred on the Feast of Shavuot, fifty days after Yeshua was crucified during Pesach in the same year 33 A.D. ***Three Thousand Jewish*** people were saved that day as the Ruach HaKodesh was poured out upon the 120 ***Jews*** in that upper room!

Sha'ul returned to Jerusalem from the nations just before Shavuot in the year 58 A.D. Twenty-five years after that first, supernatural outpouring of the Ruach HaKodesh in 33 A.D. He makes a report to the elders of the Messianic Community in Jerusalem about his successes in his ministry to the Gentiles. Those Messianic Leaders then respond to Sha'ul's ministry report.

> *"On hearing it, they praised God; but they also said to him, You see, brother, how many tens of thousands of believers there are among the Judeans, and they are all zealots for the Torah."* **Acts 21:20**

A mere twenty five years later there are ***tens of thousands of Jewish believers*** in Jerusalem alone! How did so many Jewish people receive Yeshua? They were presented the Jewish Messiah coupled with signs and wonders through the Ruach HaKodesh!

This is the model for revival! This is how we can experience Jewish Revival today! The veil and cloak disguising Yeshua must be removed so the Church may successfully share and reveal the Jewish Messiah to the Jewish People combined with the Ruach HaKodesh and with Signs and Wonders. This is how God will restore His body!

IV. The Restoration begins.

The death knoll that resulted from the Council of Nicea over 1,700 years ago also spawned a desire among some Godly men and women within the body of Messiah that seek the restoration of biblical truth. This group of people have grown stronger over the millennia becoming greater with every generation. They are passionate and zealous for God, seeking to rediscover the secrets and power of the first century body of believers. There are thousands of believers in the body of Messiah today searching for the truth!

Throughout biblical history (which is also world history) there have been numerous reformations or revivals recorded. Piece by piece, the body is being restored, like a giant jigsaw puzzle. The Body of Messiah is being restored.

Martin Luther (who became extremely Anti-Semitic in his later years after unsuccessfully trying to evangelize Jewish people) never intended to start a protestant movement. His heart was the reformation and cleansing of false theology, corruption, and indulgences from the Catholic Church[8]. A majority of church congregates in the middle ages were illiterate which led to many church sponsored abuses and grievances. When Luther tacked his "95 Thesis's" to the Church door in Wittenberg on October 31st, 1517 he sparked a spiritual revolution. Luther's bold act opened the door for the Puritans, the Calvinists (Calvin reintroduced Hebraic studies within the body for the first time in over 1,300 years) and even John Fox's Scottish reformation. This led to the Quakers and even the Church of England breaking away from Rome and Catholicism. All because one man thought that every person should be able to read the bible for themselves and that each person should ask God for the forgiveness of their own sins, and seek salvation as individuals. So many men and woman would be put to death over this reformation. Many martyrs would be made but eventually the reformation took root and people began learning to read and ingest the word of God for themselves.

The reformation revolution led to the "Great Awakening" in America in the 1750's which was a holiness and righteousness movement of repenting of Sins and turning back to God. The focus of this outpouring was a Godly lifestyle. This was followed by the Second Great Awakening that went from the 1790's through the 1840's and focused on the same principles. [9]

> *"What God wants is that you be holy, that you keep away from sexual immorality, [4]that each of you know how to manage his sexual impulses in a holy and honorable manner, [5]without giving in to lustful desires, like the pagans who don't know God"* **I Thessalonians 4:3-5**

These "Great Awakenings" followed God's pattern of revival established in Acts Chapter 3.

> *"Therefore, repent and turn to God, so that your sins may be erased"* **Acts 3:19.**

First comes the restoration of the word which occurred in Acts 3:18 followed by repentance of Sin and Salvation in Acts 3:19!

The next great wave of revival was in the later part of the 19th century through the 20th century. This outpouring of God was the restoration of the Ruach HaKodesh (Holy Spirit) that birthed the

Pentecostal and Charismatic movements[10]. The body experienced profound outpourings of the Ruach Ha Kodesh (Holy Spirit) coupled with some signs and wonders. It was the restoration of the gifts of the Spirit.

> *"Moreover, to each person is given the particular manifestation of the Spirit that will be for the common good. [8]To one, through the Spirit, is given a word of wisdom; to another, a word of knowledge, in accordance with the same Spirit; [9]to another, faith, by the same Spirit; and to another, gifts of healing, by the one Spirit; [10]to another, the working of miracles; to another, prophecy; to another, the ability to judge between spirits; to another, the ability to speak in different kinds of tongues; and to yet another, the ability to interpret tongues. [11]One and the same Spirit is at work in all these things, distributing to each person as he chooses."*
> **I Corinthians 12:7-11**

This Holy Spirit outpouring is how we are refreshed. The Ruach HaKodesh brings refreshing. This was listed next in Acts 3:20.

> *"So that times of refreshing may come from the Lord's presence."* **Acts 3:20**

In Summary, first came the restoration of the word, then repentance of Sin followed by times of refreshing through the outpouring of the Ruach HaKodesh!

Following God's pattern in Acts chapter three the next phase is restoration. Restoration is why the world is experiencing the rebirth of the Messianic Community. God has ordained the restoration of the Jewish Root, the Jewish component, the final piece of the puzzle before Yeshua returns.

"He has to remain in heaven until the time comes for restoring everything, as God said long ago, when he spoke through the holy prophets." **Acts 3:21**

Yeshua has to remain in heaven until the time for restoration. This is directly connected to Chapter Four. Yeshua cannot return until Israel says, "Blessed is He who comes in the Name of the Lord". This passage confirms Yeshua's own words in Matthew 23. Theology must reconcile to scripture! God has begun the restoration of Israel so that Israel may fulfill its prophetic calling to be a light unto the nations!

"He has said, "It is not enough that you are merely my servant to raise up the tribes of Ya'akov and restore the offspring of Isra'el. I will also make you a light to the nations, so my salvation can spread to the ends of the earth." **Isaiah 49:6**

All the revivals, reformations, and outpourings of God's Spirit over the last 1,700 years has moved the body of Messiah closer and closer to being restored and unified with Messianic Israel. Soon all things will be restored!

The restoration of true biblical culture, worship, and lifestyle is the key to provoking unsaved Israel to receive their Jewish Messiah! Believing Jews and believing Gentiles celebrating the feast days together in the Holy Spirit releases a heavenly anointing and power that draws unsaved Jewish and Gentile people alike to their Messiah, Yeshua!

Chapter Seven Notes

1. Philip Schaff, D.D., LL.D. and Henry Wace, D.D. *"NICENE AND POST-NICENE FATHERS OF THE CHRISTIAN CHURCH. SECOND SERIES VOLUME XIV"*. T&T CLARK, EDINBURGH

2. Daniels. J,L, "*Anti-Semitism in the Hellenistic-Roman Period*" JBL 98 (1979)

3. Runciman, Steven (1990). "*The Fall of Constantinople, 1453*". Cambridge University Press

4. William Smith, D.C.L., LL.D.: "*A Dictionary of Greek and Roman Antiquities*" John Murray, London, 1875

5. Dwyer, John C., "*Church history: twenty centuries of Catholic Christianity*", (1998)

6. "Paul, St." Cross, F. L., ed. The Oxford dictionary of the Christian church. New York: Oxford University Press. 2005

7. The Messiah Texts, Raphael Patai, Wayne State University, 1988

8. Plass, Ewald M. "*Monasticism,*" in What Luther Says: An Anthology. St. Louis: Concordia Publishing House, 1959

9. George Marsden, Jonathan Edwards: A Life (New Haven, Conn.: Yale University Press, 2003),

10. "*Pentecostalism*". The Columbia Encyclopedia, Sixth Edition. 2008. http://www.encyclopedia.com/doc/1E1-Pentcstl.html.

— Chapter 8 —

What Does God Want Me to Do?

I. New Wine Requires New Wineskins

> *"Also, no one puts new wine into old wineskins; if he does, the new wine will burst the skins and be spilled, and the skins too will be ruined.* [38] *On the contrary, new wine must be put into freshly prepared wineskins.* [39] *Besides that, after drinking old wine, people don't want new; because they say, `The old is good enough.'"* **Luke 5:37-39**

This reading ends Luke Chapter Five. It would appear that Yeshua's teaching about the wineskins left the Pharisee's speechless. In the beginning of Luke Chapter seven the Pharisee's are inquiring why Yeshua's talmidim are not fasting. Yeshua's reply sharply ended their questioning but why? Did they suddenly become quiet because (like the greater body of Messiah today) they were studying Greek Philosophy so they had no idea what Yeshua was talking about, or as native born Israelis (called Sabras) did they actually understand and comprehend.

Christian Theology is vexed by Hebrew idioms because contemporary bible colleges and universities teach and study scriptures through a Hellenistic viewpoint and context vice the Jewish culture and context in which it was written. Christianity has unsuccessfully grappled with Yeshua's New Wine teaching and other Hebrew Idioms for millennium. The general consensus of Christian Commentaries is that the new garment is the Church and Grace while the old garment is Israel and the Law and done away with. Similarly, the new wine represents the New Testament and the Church while the old wineskin represents the Old Testament and Israel.

The misunderstanding of this idiom reveals the essence of the friction between Christianity and the Messianic movement. This explains why such a large chasm has existed between the two for over 1,700 years and accounts for so little unity between Jewish and Gentile believers. Contemporary theology teaches that the Old and the New are incompatible, that the Old Testament and Israel is incompatible with Christianity and the New Testament. The old is obsolete and done away with so by default the Church and Gentiles becomes a new, separate, independent entity estranged from the national life of Israel. This is the seed of Church Replacement Theology and Anti Semitism within the greater body.

There is one word to sum up this type of interpretation or theology: "un-reconcilable". To reconcile something is to bring it into agreement or harmony; to make it compatible or consistent: to reconcile differing statements. Yeshua's remarks in Luke 5:39 make contemporary theology and commentaries concerning the new wine and new wine skins un-reconcilable to scripture.

> *"Besides that, after drinking old wine, people don't want new; because they say, `The old is good enough'"* **Luke 5:39**

Yeshua's statement here creates a profound dilemma if you are to believe contemporary theological commentaries because they don't reconcile with the words of Yeshua. If the "Church" is the "new wine" then Yeshua's is actually saying; "The Temple, Pharisee's, and Sadducees are a wonderful wine and nobody wants the new wine (church) after they have drunk of the old! This error is all too common in modern Biblical Hermeneutics. Another prime example is:

> "Don't think that I have come to abolish the Torah or the Prophets. I have come not to abolish but to complete. [18]Yes indeed! I tell you that until heaven and earth pass away, not so much as a yud or a stroke will pass from the Torah— not until everything that must happen has happened. [19]So whoever disobeys the least of these mitzvot and teaches others to do so will be called the least in the Kingdom of Heaven. But whoever obeys them and so teaches will be called great in the Kingdom of Heaven." **Matthew 5:17-19**

I have discussed and argued just about every religious teaching and position presented by Christian Scholars that the Old Testament has been done away with and that Yeshua "nailed the Old Testament to the cross". But like the new wine in Luke 5:39, this theology has a serious and significant flaw. First and foremost neither Yeshua, His talmidim, or the scripture ever make the statement "The Old Testament is done away with" or "The Old Testament was nailed to the cross". Second, this teaching is un-reconcilable with Yeshua's own words that you just read in Matthew 5. So who's in error? The scholars teaching that the Old Testament is done away with or the words of Yeshua who said it isn't? Basic hermeneutics must be applied to every teaching and theology.

Pause to think and dwell on the next few sentences for a few moments. The term "scriptures" is used in the New Testament some 130 times! Yeshua, Peter, Paul, and James to name just a few New Testament figures routinely refer to the "Scriptures" in their teachings and writings! II Timothy 3:16 relates that **ALL SCRIPTURE** is inspired by God, or God breathed and valuable for teaching truth, convicting of sin, correcting faults, and teaching in righteousness! When all of the references to "scripture" were made the New Testament (B'rith Hadasha) didn't exist yet. The Canonized New Testament was still over 300 years in the future! What "Scripture" were they all talking about? The Tanach (Hebrew for Old Testament). The Talmidim of Yeshua radically evangelized their world only using the Tanach! Your teaching and theology must reconcile with scripture or it's in ERROR! Paul confirmed Yeshua's words and gave great clarity to the fact that the Torah and Tanach has *not* been done away with for either Jews or Gentiles.

> *"For it is not merely the hearers of Torah whom God considers righteous; rather, it is the doers of what Torah says who will be made righteous in God's sight. [14]For whenever Gentiles, who have no Torah, do naturally what the Torah requires, then these, even though they don't have Torah, for themselves are Torah".* **Romans 2:13-14**

Paul declares that it's not the one who hears Torah, it's the one who does what Torah says that are made righteous in God's sight! It's almost impossible for a person who has received religious training or attended seminary to receive a new teaching from heaven. This is exactly why Yeshua chose men who knew God's word but were not religiously trained for His talmidim.

There were many iconic and famous theologians alive 2,000 years ago, all of whom Yeshua ignored when He was choosing His disciples. Why, because they were religiously trained, they were old wine skins who couldn't receive the New Wine! The new is rejected by the old; history proves this to be true. The last group to receive new wine from God is the first group to persecute the next ones who receive new wine; they quickly become old wine skins and won't receive the new wine.

A common mistake that many believers make is assuming that Yeshua's talmidim were ignorant, simple, untrained people with no education. A typical primary Jewish education in Yeshua's time started at the age of 4-5 years old and involved extensive memorization of Torah. Fishermen and tax collectors received fundamental training in Torah which was limited to reading and memorizing the word, little or no theology was taught. They were new wineskins awaiting a new wine. One of the famous Jewish theologians that was alive when Yeshua walked the earth was Gamaliel. Sha'ul refers to Gamaliel as his mentor and teacher. Gamaliel is still a highly regarded sage within the Orthodox Jewish Community today. A member of the Sanhedrin in Jerusalem 2,000 years ago, Gamaliel's name is mentioned twice in scripture. Once for giving sound advice to the Sanhedrin regarding the teachings of Yeshua's disciples and the other for being the teacher of Sha'ul:

> *"But one member had a different perspective. He was a Pharisee named Gamaliel, who was an expert on religious law and was very popular with the people. He stood up and ordered that the apostles be sent outside the council chamber for a while."* **Acts 5:34**

> *"So my advice is, leave these men alone. If they are teaching and doing these things merely on their own, it will soon be overthrown. 39But if it is of God, you will not be able to stop them. You may even find yourselves fighting against God."* **Acts 5: 38-39**

"I am a Jew, born in Tarsus, a city in Cilicia, and I was brought up and educated here in Jerusalem under Gamaliel. At his feet I learned to follow our Jewish laws and customs very carefully. I became very zealous to honor God in everything I did, just as all of you are today." **Acts 22:3**

Yeshua specifically chose those non-religious trained fishermen and tax collectors over theologians because they lacked the bias and closed mindedness that formal religion teaches. Even then, He had to help the Talmidim understand!

"Then he opened their minds, so that they could understand the Tanakh" **Luke 24:45**

If you want to experience a new, supernatural wine you must be transformed into a new supernatural wine skin so that you may receive the New Wine. The "One New Man" understanding and concept is most definitely a heavenly new wine!

II. Something different.

For 1,700 years there have been two streams, two houses of worship; Messianic Jewish synagogues and the Gentile Church. An overwhelming majority of Messianic Jewish Books and Publications to date are Hebrew Roots teachings. They contain a plethora of weighty, deep, and nourishing Torah based teachings straight from the olive tree root that Christians love and seek. There is nothing wrong with that. The Messianic teachings are wildly popular because they go beyond the shallow facade presented by most Christians. The DNA of the natural branch matches the olive tree roots DNA so the Messianic teaching reflects that deep nourishment, the ancient knowledge and understanding drawn directly from the olive tree root. This is a necessary and important step in the final restoration but there is so much more.

You've read the history of America and the biblical principles of its foundation in the opening chapters. God birthed America as a nation with a prophetic destiny and calling to be the "One New Man" to release this end time teaching of Messianic Jew and believing Gentile (Christian) reconciliation to the world. You've learned how and why the body of Messiah has gotten to the place of apostasy and death. You've read what God expects of you and me, Yeshua's Ambassadors here on the earth. You've read God's plan and now know what it should look like, and why. God does NOT purpose that we (Messianic Israel and the Church) acknowledge each other's existence and remain divided into two separate houses. His written word gives great clarity to this topic. He is birthing something drastically new and different then what exists today in the greater body of Messiah. God is pouring out new wine which requires new wine skins. He is birthing "oneness", the Jewish bride for His Son the Jewish Groom. This "One New Man" relationship of unity between believing Jew and believing Gentile is similar to the relationship between a man and wife.

> *"For this reason, a man should leave his father and mother and be united with his wife."* **Mark 10:7**

When a man and woman get married they become echad (Hebrew for complete, one!). A man and wife are united, one, they are complete. Yet the man does not become a woman nor does the woman become a man.

> *"There is neither Jew nor Gentile, neither slave nor freeman, neither male nor female; for in union with the Messiah Yeshua, you are all one."* **Galatians 3:28**

In the "One New Man" unification a Jew does not become a Gentile and a Gentile does not become a Jew. Both Jew and Gentile retain their cultural identity. The two become one like the bridegroom and bride! When a man and woman get married they don't live in separate houses across the street from each other, occasionally waiving at each other, acknowledging each other's existence, and occasionally having a reconciliation meeting! When a man and woman are married they come together as one under the same roof. They share finances and food, they work through their difficulties together, celebrate their victories together, and live a covenant life together as one.

This relationship will take tears, work, humility, and prayer. The Messianic Community can't Judiaize and the Church can't convert. This reminds me of an old Messianic saying:

"For 1,700 years the Church has been trying to graft the Jews into a Christmas Tree vice Olive Tree!"

Jew and Gentile must meet in the middle! We're both serving the same God, the same Messiah, and the same Holy Spirit while remembering that it was God who birthed and created the biblical culture of Israel and the Jewish people into which He would birth His Son, Yeshua the Jew! We the bride of this Jewish groom await His return in which a Jewish wedding will occur and we'll go with our groom to our home in Jerusalem. This understanding will cause some of my Messianic colleagues to be upset with me and undoubtedly numerous Pastors and clergy as well. I am active in and support the Messianic Movement. It is truly a prophetic, end-time move of God! I also love my Christian brothers and sisters in the Church who have faithfully carried forth the Gospel around the world. But there's so much more to gain if we will tear down the wall of separation and become one, literally!

The absolute truth of God's word will set us free and restore the power and anointing of His presence back into our congregations if we submit to God and His word and become ONE! Not two expressions or streams of faith

Paul said he was "all things to all people". I am blessed to have the wonderful opportunity of routinely speaking in churches across America and around the world. I have spoken in just about every Christian denomination (even Catholic and Baptist denominations who traditionally do not permit speakers outside of their denomination) including non-denomination, Charismatic, Pentecostal, Evangelical, and various ecumenical conferences. I adapt my presentation and my language to match whatever denomination I'm speaking at so that they will receive the message at their place of understanding. My question is this; Can you do the same with the Jewish people? Pastor, can you share a teaching or message in your local synagogue or Messianic Congregation in a Jewish setting and context? In almost 15 years of ministry I've not met a Pastor or Christian teacher who can answer yes contrary to Romans 1:15 which emphatically states that we are to share the Gospel "to the Jew first".

II. Pride of Ministry

I want to speak frankly for a moment to every Messianic Rabbi, Pastor, Congregation Leader, Clergy, and individual who is involved in any type of Kingdom ministry. I want to share with you a word from God that pierced my own heart several years ago: "It's not your ministry". You have a calling that God has equipped you to do. These callings come in many different venues and expressions, but it's not yours. It's God's ministry and must conform to His word and will!

Every living human being has an appointment with death, just one! When you stand before your creator and judge, the ministry you performed here on earth won't be with you, it will remain here on the earth. If you're unable to lay down that ministry for the greater Kingdom of God and His plans, if you're unwilling to change your ministry to conform it to God's word then you're in control and God isn't. If you're in control your ministry is man-made, based on pride which God calls an Idol, a golden calf.

Pride of ministry is one of the greatest hindrances to unity and God's will. Pride of Ministry causes division; it offends the Ruach HaKodesh causing His presence to depart which results in spiritually dead congregations and Churches.

> *"Greedy dogs, never satisfied—such are the shepherds, unable to understand; they all turn to their own way, each one intent on his own gain."* **Isaiah 56:11**

Time is running out. Collectively, the greater body of Messiah must begin working together according to God's word for God's Kingdom. The Body of Messiah must stop building personal empires of ministry!

III. Staying In Tune with God's Covenants.

This is an absolute biblical truth; Yeshua is not coming back for the "Bride", a culturally Jewish bride, a spotless unified bride that is intimate with Him, His family, and His culture!

> *"Let us rejoice and be glad! Let us give him the glory! For the time has come for the wedding of the Lamb, and his Bride has prepared herself."* **Revelation 19:7**

The greater body of Messiah must submit its self to God's word and will. It's time for the bride to prepare herself for her Jewish groom. The world hasn't experienced a global outpouring of God or received Yeshua as Messiah globally because we haven't fulfilled Yeshua's Command in John 17 to be one! Jewish and

Gentile believers in Yeshua are currently in two separate camps but this is starting to change! When it reaches its fullness we'll see and experience worldwide revival.

I believe this book is a clarion call to all believers to hear the watchman's shofar and prepare! The world we live in today seems to be falling apart at the seams, including America. A two state solution has been presented to Israel and the Arab Nations in the Middle East and is being forced upon Israel by America, the United Nations, and the European Union. God's judgment is about to be unleashed upon America for this unbiblical act.

I have dedicated a significant portion of my life (I retired from the Unites States Navy after serving 22 years, specifically I served on Fast Attack Submarines) in service to the defense of this country. There are few who are more patriotic and love this Republic more than I, but America is a temporary place for us! We who belong to Messiah Yeshua are citizens of an even greater Kingdom whose King commands us to focus on that Kingdom! We are sojourners here, we're just passing through this world so don't become preoccupied with or overly attached to it!

Many ministries are engaged in many battles regarding the spiritual and moral corruption of this country. We should be praying against evil, but programs, events, and seminars can't become "Idols" which hinder or even prevent followers from fulfilling God's will. Are you praying to preserve this corrupted way of life so you're comfortable American lifestyle won't change or are you repenting for being part of this morally bankrupt nation and seeking the Lord for His forgiveness? These are two very diverse, very different strategies and thought processes. Repentance is from God, preserving the morally corrupt is not!

Read very carefully as what I'm about to share can be taken out of context and misunderstood. God commands us to take a stand against evil but it's not the ultimate judgment of the world. Those who are involved in evil practices and idolatry simply have no place in the Kingdom to come:

> *"Don't you know that unrighteous people will have no share in the Kingdom of God? Don't delude yourselves—people who engage in sex before marriage, who worship idols, who engage in sex after marriage with someone other than their spouse, who engage in active or passive homosexuality, [10]who steal, who are greedy, who get drunk, and who assail people with contemptuous language, who rob—none of them will share in the Kingdom of God. [11]Some of you used to do these things. But you have cleansed yourselves, you have been set apart for God, you have come to be counted righteous through the power of the Lord Yeshua the Messiah and the Spirit of our God."* **I Corinthians 6:9-11**

There are many today who profess to be Christians but are still engaged in abominable practices. They have no share in the Kingdom to Come. You cannot engage in sinful behavior and think you're included in the Kingdom of God because you attend a weekly service somewhere. The greater body of Messiah has already been deceived and the great Apostasy, the great falling away from God has begun. Many Congregations, individuals, and clergy are involved in these practices and truly believe that they are saved and going to heaven, they are trapped by a delusion of Satan! These people are "luke warm" because they believe there is nothing wrong. Yeshua said He will vomit them out of His mouth!

Matthew 25 reveals a great hidden mystery of what is specifically on God's heart and mind. The scriptural metric used for the judgment of the nations is recorded in Yeshua's own words and is quite different from I Corinthians 6:9-11.

> *"When the Son of Man comes in his glory, accompanied by all the angels, he will sit on his glorious throne. 32All the nations will be assembled before him, and he will separate people one from another as a shepherd separates sheep from goats. 33The `sheep' he will place at his right hand and the `goats' at his left. 34Then the King will say to those on his right, `Come, you whom my Father has blessed, take your inheritance, the Kingdom prepared for you from the founding of the world. 35For I was hungry and you gave me food, I was thirsty and you gave me something to drink, I was a stranger and you made me your guest, 36I needed clothes and you provided them, I was sick and you took care of me, I was in prison and you visited me.' 37Then the people who have done what God wants will reply, Lord, when did we see you hungry and feed you, or thirsty and give you something to drink? 38When did we see you a stranger and make you our guest or needing clothes and provide them? 39When did we see you sick or in prison, and visit you? 40The King will say to them, `Yes! I tell you that whenever you did these things for one of the least important of these brothers of mine, you did them for me!"* **Matthew 25:31-40**

The standard used in judging the nations is Israel. Many believers are focused on personal quality of life, comfort level, and material possessions while Yeshua told us to do the exact opposite.

> *"But seek first his Kingdom and his righteousness, and all these things will be given to you as well."* **Matthew 6:33**

In Yeshua's own words this is how the final judgment will unfold which is not man-made eschatology, it's the written word contained in every one of your bibles regardless of the translation. Even inaccurate and poorly translated bibles have not changed this metric:

> *"Up, Zion! Escape, you who dwell with the daughter of Babylon. [8]For thus says the Lord of hosts: He sent Me after glory, to the nations which plunder you; for he who touches you touches the apple of His eye. [9]For surely I will shake My hand against them, and they shall become spoil for their servants. Then you will know that the Lord of hosts has sent me."* **Zechariah 2:7-9**

Those who seek to plunder Israel (take or divide Israel's inheritance, the Land) are touching the Apple of God's eye and He will raise His hand against them!

> *"When that day comes, I will make Yerushalayim a heavy stone for all the peoples. All who try to lift it will hurt themselves, and all the earth's nations will be massed against her."* **Zechariah 12:3**

Don't fall into Satan's trap of praying against God's word. Read carefully, this scripture in Zechariah 12:3 states "**ALL THE EARTHS NATIONS**" including America will be judged according to Yeshua's words in Matthew 25. I know this is strong and some might become anxious, even worried about this but the words are not mine, they're God's. He established the metric for judgment not Messianic Jews, not Orthodox Jews, Not Christians, and not theologians. The body of Messiah can no longer pretend these events will happen somewhere else but not here in America. America is not above God's word nor has it replaced Israel or the Kingdom of God. Deceptive and false doctrine is occurring within the body because people, clergy, nations, and leaders do not know the word of God!

When Yeshua returns the Kingdom of God will be established here on the earth and Jerusalem which will once again be the center and focus of the world, not America, not the 57 Islamic States, not the European Union and the United Nations, but God's holy city of Jerusalem!

IV. Is God Done with America?

To answer the question that is asked in the title of this book: "Is God done with America?" I don't believe so, not yet! America has yet to fulfill its prophetic destiny, to invoke and release the One New Man across America and the world. This is God's plan to restore life back to the dead church. The Greater body of Messiah will understand the culture and context of what it's grafted into! Whole scale restoration of the body of Messiah will begin as the body matures and biblical truth is restored back into the church. The church will then begin provoking Israel to jealousy. Israel will on a national level begin to receive Yeshua their Messiah. When the native branch is grafted back into the olive tree it will be life from the dead. This life in turn sparks a worldwide revival as Messianic Israel will call out to Yeshua to return and be their King. Then we, the greater body of Messiah comprised of Messianic Jews and Believing Gentiles, will enter in to the wedding feast with the Lamb, our Jewish Groom, Yeshua! Oh what a glorious day this will be! This is the reason that God has released this awakening within the greater body regarding it's Jewish roots, culture, and heritage. It's not to impress Christians with deep Hebrew teachings and revelation. The last great move of God is His Biblical plan of restoring the bride (Jewish and Gentile believers) for the return of their Jewish groom and celebrate the Jewish wedding feast!

America stands at a critical crossroads of spiritual choice. Will America choose the God of Isaac or the god of Ishmael? Will

America seek revival and a return to God and His word or will America continue to pursue Secular Humanism and turn away from Him? God will be done with America if America does not pray, repent and turn back to Him! If America refuses to fulfill its heavenly destiny God will choose another nation while America will lose the blessings of God and like Great Britain begin its descent to the ash heap of former empires and nations that only exist today in the annuls of history.

V. The Challenge.

Change will come when the greater body of Messiah submits to God's word and plans vice our own. It is a journey that will take us "Back to the Future". The Kingdom to come is revealed in the Kingdom of One, Yeshua! God established and Yeshua defined the biblical and cultural model to follow! Let's do what Yeshua the Jew did!

I wish to leave you with a few challenges as I close. I pray that having read this book you are not the same person you were when you started it. My hope and prayer is that Israel might be saved and that you will be the vehicle of Jewish Revival God desires. I pray that you have a new or renewed passion to see the face of God, to have the natural invaded by the supernatural from heaven. I don't have all the answers but I have an open and willing heart and mind to let God do His will and His work. God desires that you be a holy revolutionary in your faith, your Church or Messianic Synagogue. Will you be the One New Man?

I challenge you to read your bible daily. Be like the good people of Berea and search out the word. The truth will set you free and you will not be fooled by false theologies or false messiahs. God's word stands on its own and speaks for itself! God's blessings and promises are for you *if* you are obedient to Him.

I challenge you to begin sharing the "Good News" with unsaved Jewish people. This necessitates a cultural paradigm shift to be effective. Every Messianic Ministry in America today will gladly help you in this endeavor to fulfill Gods calling. If you can't find a resource, contact my office and I will come to your Church or Congregation. We all must work to "hasten" Yeshua's return!

I challenge you to begin celebrating the Biblical feast days vice man-made holidays. Teaching is head knowledge, celebrating them is a matter of the heart. Remember

> *"For it is not merely the hearers of Torah whom God considers righteous; rather, it is the doers of what Torah says who will be made righteous in God's sight."* **Romans 2:13**

The feast days place you and the body of Messiah back into alignment with God's calendar and timeline. You'll celebrate the feasts when Yeshua returns so rehearse them now so you'll be ready! Remember Gentiles, few things pique the interest of Jewish person more than a Gentile who is celebrating the Lord's feast days! Scripture does not record Jewish holidays. This is the starting point to "provoke Jewish people to jealousy". It's the seed of oneness!

I challenge you to become "Messianic Jewish" focused and centered in all that you do for the Kingdom of God. Remember Romans 1:16; "To the Jew First". Stop Church Replacement Theology and teach awareness to others to do the same. Replacement Theology is Satan's deceitful plan to divide Jew and Gentile, divide the land, and attempt to stop Yeshua's return. Remember, Satan is trying to steal YOUR inheritance, it can only be done if the strong man (you) is bound. Don't squander your inheritance! Write letters to the editor in your local newspaper in support of Israel. Call or write your Congressperson or Senator and tell them to support Israel. Demand that your denomination support Messianic Israel or find one that does! Talk to your Church and Pastors council and share the "One New Man" message with them! Invite Messianic Speakers and Psalmists to your congregation and bless and support them! Take a tour to Israel. Buy Israeli products! Seek out and support your local Messianic Jewish synagogue or Congregation, they desperately need your help and support spiritually, physically, and financially! As I'm writing this over 68% of Americans when polled support Israel, the people are ready.

I challenge you to put your money where your heart is. I have included Appendix A at the end of this book that lists Messianic Jewish Ministries at work in America and Israel that you, your church, or congregation can and should support. Not one single penny should go to any ministry in Israel or a ministry supporting Israel that does not have Messianic Jewish support and involvement. This stand speaks louder than words to Israel and the Jewish community regarding the Messianic Jewish Movement and the body of Messiah's commitment to it. It holds ministries accountable to God's word. It will also change the political and spiritual face of Israel. Your money talks, teach it to speak Messianic!

> *"For it has been the good pleasure of Macedonia and Achaia to make a certain contribution for the poor among the holy ones who are at Yerushalayim. [27] Yes, it has been their good pleasure, and they are their debtors. For if the Goyim have been made partakers of their spiritual things, they owe it to them also to serve them in fleshly things."* **Romans 15:26-27**

Lastly, I challenge you to fan your flames of Passion for God! THERE IS NO SUBSTITUTE FOR PASSION. Passion is the fuel of your will! If you want God bad enough, if you desire His presence above all the other things of this world, you'll receive the presence of God into your life, He will come! Passion will do more to change the body of Messiah than any program, seminar, or meeting! Passion will change you and you congregation. If you'll follow Godly passion vice of man-made religion and doctrine you'll become a world changer. May we hear Israel cry out "Blessed is He who comes in the name of the Lord".

There is one person in this world that can make a difference, YOU! May the Living God of Israel bless you and keep you!

Rabbi Eric & Barb Carlson

Rabbi Eric Carlson is founder and shepherd of Congregation Zion's Sake located in Newport News, Va. Congregation Zion's Sake is a Messianic Congregation where Jew and Gentile break down the wall of enmity and worship together as "One in Messiah". Through a prophetic vision from God he is called to spread the "Good News" of the Jewish Messiah according to Romans 1:16: "To the Jew First", to provoke the Jewish people to jealousy, and to reach the lost and hurting among the Nations.

Eric is a native of Fairview, Pennsylvania. He attained the rank of Senior Chief Petty Officer in the United States Navy, retiring in August 2003 after 22 years of decorated service in the Submarine Force. Responding to God's call he founded Congregation Zion's Sake in May 2000 and entered full time ministry upon retiring from Naval Service.

Rabbi Carlson was ordained by the International Alliance of Messianic Congregations and Synagogues (IAMCS) in January 2006 after two years of Messianic Yeshiva.

Eric hosts a daily Radio program "Torah Chai" on the Oasis Network 91.5 FM in Tidewater, Va., 89.7 FM and 93.7 FM in Branson/Springfield, Missouri and 88.7 FM in Canton, Ohio.

Eric is married to the former Barbara Patterson of Altoona, Pa. Barb teaches Israeli and Messianic Worship Dance and leads the Congregation Zion's Sake Dance Team. She has led her Dance team on several mission trips to Russia and Siberia. Barb teaches dance nationally at the MJAA South Eastern Conference, the M.J.A.A. (Messianic Jewish Alliance of America) National Conferences, and U.M.J.C. (Union of Messianic Jewish Congregations) National Conferences. Eric and Barb have 4 children (Amy 26, Jendi 23 married to Joshua Thompson, Tyler 20, and Erica 15) and three Grandchildren (Eliana, Malachi, and Aviel). Eric and Barb currently reside in York County, Virginia.

Congregation Zion's Sake
1233 Shields Rd
Newport News, VA 23608
Ph# 757-874-3303
www.zionsake.org

APPENDIX A
Messianic Jewish Ministries.

Congregation Zion's Sake
1233 Shields Rd
Newport News, VA 23608
Phone: (757) 873-3303
Fax: (757) 874-2040
www.zionsake.org

Sid Roth's "Messianic Vision"
P. O. Box 1918
Brunswick, GA 31521
Phone: (912) 265-2500
Fax: (912) 265-3735
www.sidroth.org

Promise Keepers
P.O. Box 11798
Denver, CO 80211-0798
Phone: 1-866-PROMISE (1-866-776-6473)
www.promisekeepers.org

Dugit
Messianic Outreach
P.O. Box 11174
Tel Aviv 61111
Phone: +972 (0)3-621-2108
www.dugit.org

M.J.A.A. (Messianic Jewish Alliance of America)
PO BOX 274
Springfield, PA 19064
Phone: (800) 225-6522
Fax: (610) 338-0471
www.mjaa.org

I.A.M.C.S. (International Alliance of Messianic Congregations and Synagogues)
P.O. Box 1570
Havertown, PA 19083
Phone: 215-425-5590 or 1-866-IAMCS-NOW (toll free) (1-866-426-2766)
www.iamcs.org

Jewish Voice
Jonathan Bernis
P.O. Box 81439
Phoenix, AZ 85069-1439.
Phone: (800) 424-0408
www.jewishvoice.org

Jewish Jewels
Neil and Jamie Lash
P.O. Box 450550
Fort Lauderdale, FL 33345
www.jewishjewels.org

Jezreel
18 Kairnes Street
Albany, NY 12205
Phone: 518-438-4370
www.jezreelinternational.org

U.M.J.C. (Union of Messianic Jewish Congregations)
529 Jefferson St. NE
Albuquerque, NM 87108
Phone: 800-692-8652
www.umjc.org

BUY A SHARE OF THE FUTURE IN YOUR COMMUNITY

These certificates make great holiday, graduation and birthday gifts that can be personalized with the recipient's name. The cost of one S.H.A.R.E. or one square foot is $54.17. The personalized certificate is suitable for framing and will state the number of shares purchased and the amount of each share, as well as the recipient's name. The home that you participate in "building" will last for many years and will continue to grow in value.

Here is a sample SHARE certificate:

HABITAT FOR HUMANITY

THIS CERTIFIES THAT

YOUR NAME HERE

HAS INVESTED IN A HOME FOR A DESERVING FAMILY

1985-2005

TWENTY YEARS OF BUILDING FUTURES IN OUR COMMUNITY ONE HOME AT A TIME

1200 SQUARE FOOT HOUSE @ $65,000 = $54.17 PER SQUARE FOOT
This certificate represents a tax deductible donation. It has no cash value.

YES, I WOULD LIKE TO HELP!

*I support the work that Habitat for Humanity does and I want to be part of the excitement! As a donor, I will receive periodic updates on your construction activities but, more importantly, I know my gift will help a family in our community realize the dream of homeownership. **I would like to SHARE in your efforts against substandard housing in my community!** (Please print below)*

PLEASE SEND ME _____ SHARES at $54.17 EACH = $ $_____

In Honor Of: _____

Occasion: (Circle One) HOLIDAY   BIRTHDAY   ANNIVERSARY

OTHER: _____

Address of Recipient: _____

Gift From: _____ *Donor Address:* _____

Donor Email: _____

I AM ENCLOSING A CHECK FOR $ $_____ PAYABLE TO HABITAT FOR HUMANITY **OR** PLEASE CHARGE MY VISA OR MASTERCARD *(CIRCLE ONE)*

Card Number _____ Expiration Date: _____

Name as it appears on Credit Card _____ Charge Amount $ _____

Signature _____

Billing Address _____

Telephone # Day _____ Eve _____

PLEASE NOTE: Your contribution is tax-deductible to the fullest extent allowed by law.
Habitat for Humanity • P.O. Box 1443 • Newport News, VA 23601 • 757-596-5553
www.HelpHabitatforHumanity.org